Garage Criticism

Garage Criticism:

Cultural Missives in an Age
of Distraction

※　※　※

PETER BABIAK

ANVIL PRESS / VANCOUVER

Anvil Press Publishers Inc.
P.O. Box 3008, Main Post Office
Vancouver, B.C. V6B 3X5 CANADA
www.anvilpress.com

Library and Archives Canada Cataloguing in Publication

Babiak, Peter (Peter Roman), author
    Garage criticism : cultural missives in an age of distraction
/ Peter Babiak.

ISBN 978-1-77214-050-7 (paperback)

    1. Criticism. 2. Popular culture. I. Title.

PS8603.A258A6 2016   C814'.6   C2016-903942-0

Printed and bound in Canada
Cover design by Derek von Essen
Interior by HeimatHouse
Represented in Canada by Publishers Group Canada
Distributed by Raincoast Books

The publisher gratefully acknowledges the financial assistance of the Canada Council for the Arts, the Canada Book Fund, and the Province of British Columbia through the B.C. Arts Council and the Book Publishing Tax Credit.

To Amber Anne, for the hours of dialogue,
to Cairo, for all those hours in the garage,
and to Laura, for the best hours.

TABLE OF CONTENTS

Come Back Inside, Ponyboy; Camus Has Been Waiting

I know this thirteen-year-old kid whose English teacher assigned his class *The Outsiders*, that touchstone in the literary formation of so many adolescents. "What do you think of it?" I asked. "It's okay," he said, "I like the fight scenes, the rumbles, but there could've been more," which is probably a predictable response, though I'm sure he doesn't call fighting "rumbling" but uses a word more suited to the happily bombastic world of *Call of Duty* and *World of Warcraft*. When I asked what he thought the novel was about—specifically, that enigmatic line in Johnny's letter to Ponyboy at the end—he said "'stay gold' means you should stay young and innocent." It was an archetypal Grade 8 response, guiltlessly languid and delightfully naïve, one that I would have offered when I had to read the book when I was his age.

The Outsiders is a classic coming-of-age story about two groups of kids—two classes, really, or "cliques" if you want to use that horribly pronounced euphemism—in Tulsa, Oklahoma. The "Socs" are the rich kids from the west side of town, and the "Greasers" are the poorer ones from the east side. The story is narrated by fourteen-year-old greaser, Ponyboy Curtis, who, like most teens, is prone to identity crises and moments of existential angst. It's been a cornerstone of what today we call "young adult" lit for almost half a century, and for good reason. It's an audacious novel written *for* teens *by* a teen. Susan Eloise Hinton wrote it when she was a fifteen-year-old student at Will Rogers High in Tulsa, and published it two years later, in 1967, which is kind of remarkable when you think about it. I recently came across a University of Minnesota teacher's guide in which I read that more than 90 percent of all secondary English classes in the U.S. use *The Outsiders* every year, and even here in BC it's still listed, along with six other titles, within the "range of literature and level of challenge appropriate for students in Grade 8" in the Ministry of Education's *Performance Standards*. Which is even more remarkable.

But what exactly are we teaching when we teach a novel like *The Outsiders*? Is it the importance of knowing that if you "get smart ... nothing can touch you"? Is it, more cryptically, that gem about "staying gold" or, like Cherry the Soc girl tells Ponyboy, that "nothing is real with us," whatever that philosophical gem might mean to an adolescent brain? We empathize with the disadvantaged Greasers, of course, but are we supposed to think that being poor—an "outsider"—is a good and fine thing, and is that what we want kids to think of the novel? What exactly could it mean to be an "outsider" to a generation of readers who, like the happily wired kid I know, are relatively affluent and spend most of their time *inside* playing video games?

The Outsiders, which didn't sell well when it was first published, was about to go out of print until one publisher—Dell—noticed that teachers were putting in orders for classes. I don't know what it would have been like teaching the novel in the countercultural 1960s but I imagine a lot of teachers hoped it would engage kids and make them feel more comfortable in the awkward skins of their social misfitery, irrespective of whether that skin was economically or psychologically battered. I do remember reading the novel late in the next decade and I remember that it was somewhere in the 156 pages of that red paperback that this reading business, this thinking about words and what they do and why they're important and how, started kind of making sense to me.

Like my thirteen-year-old friend and anybody else who's ever experienced the tribalism of a high-school cafeteria, I understood that the two cliques were at the core of the novel but I probably thought the fighting between them was more entertaining than a symptom of some class antagonism that existed in the real world. Greasers and Socs were like Capulets and Montagues, Sharks and Jets, East End boys and West End girls, or Gryffindor and Slytherin: they clash, there's an entertaining and sometimes tragic struggle to get beyond the problems, and then a resolution involving some deep thought about how people are all pretty much the same—"Maybe the two different worlds we lived in weren't so different. We saw the same sunset"—but was it ever nice to see the underdogs get the upper hand, even though that hardly ever happens outside of novels and movies.

"A greaser," Hinton once said, "always lives on the outside and needs to watch his back." I admit that as the son of an autoworker and a cleaning lady, I loved to think of myself as a socially ostracized "outsider" who, like Ponyboy and his brothers Darrel and Sodapop, lived a tough life in a rougher part of town. I didn't have the cultural capital of being orphaned like them, but I created a mostly fictional concept of my own outsider status. Once I was arrested for stealing a car, I hung out with guys who smoked, had long hair and planned on staying in school only until they landed factory jobs, and I went to the "wop" school, where we called the better-off kids at the WASP schools "cakes" because that's what the Italians, who dominated my neighbourhood, called people with names like Smith and Matthews, but I wasn't impoverished. Still, what I took from *The Outsiders* in Mr. Wagman's English class is that marginalized people—working immigrant classes no less than the three orphaned guys in Tulsa—were poorer but tougher and just way more cool. Over the years the romanticized outsider theme I pulled from Hinton's novel was replaced by darker, more sophisticated books about understanding the importance of human life in light of existential precepts and the brutal fact of mortality by Nietzsche, Kafka and Camus, but my adolescence would have been very different without the romanticized myth I took away from Hinton's novel.

At thirteen, the need to embrace my inner Ponyboy and iden-tify as a rebellious misfit was no different than how most kids navigate their way between identity and authority when they're growing up. Hasn't every teen wanted to be an "outsider" since James Dean popularized that character trope in *Rebel without a Cause* in 1955, and isn't that characterization, whether rooted in real economic disenfranchisement or some subjective malaise that kids are bullied over these days, a defensive mechanism kids invoke because they need to make an impression but ultimately just want to fit in? My nephew, a super nice kid who's getting pushed around because his cultural interests are at odds with the other guys in his grade, who are all into the faux gangsta thing, tells me he's an "outsider," and the rehearsed pride in his voice indicates that although he'd probably love to be invited to the cool kids' table, he's okay biding his time on the fringe for now. He's making the best of the situation. Like Dr. Seuss's *The Cat in the Hat*—where the fish who represents conventional morality tells the boy narrator to put the cat outside—my nephew is con-sciously siding with that wonderfully Nietzschean cat, who represents that urgent need for undertaking impressive recalcitrant actions when faced with the nastiness of a social system that works by scapegoating people and, in effect, separating insiders from outsiders. I'm sure it wouldn't do my nephew any good if I told him that clever French philosophers like Jacques Derrida say that this separation is the beginning of thinking—"To keep the outside out. This is the inaugural gesture of 'logic' itself"— but this bullying that pushes him out is not only like a primal scene in adolescence but also part of our mental DNA.

I've heard that older kids, too, fabricate their outsider status as a theatrical coping mechanism, basically to fit in by putting themselves "outside." I have a current student writing a paper on it. She tells me some of her classmates in art school made a point of attaching a mental illness to themselves—OCD, ADD and bipolar were the most popular—because eccentric psychological bling comes in handy in their world. Who knows? Maybe on one of their journeys on Tumblr they came across van Gogh's meme-worthy line, "A lot of artists are mentally ill—it's a life which, to put it mildly, makes one an outsider," or heard Taylor Swift say, after recording her "haters gonna hate" song, that "not fitting in" isn't so bad. It "shows you to keep doing you, keep being you, keep trying to figure out where you fit in in the world, and eventually you will." It's pretty to think so, yet it's probably not true, but then who has time for epistemological certainty when a kid's self-esteem is at stake? In any case, though being an outsider resonates with younger people today, I wonder if that's not bound to change soon given that so many of them literally live inside, online. Earlier this year newspapers reported that words for natural things (like "acorn," "clover," "magpie" and "ox") were dropped from the *Oxford Junior Dictionary* and replaced by inside words like "blog" and "broadband." It's just dumb to think this isn't going to make kids spend even more time inside on screens, become more isolated, depressed, out of shape, and care less for the outside world than for their pixelated fictions.

I get that the "outsider" is the special province of young people; a necessary fiction that they use in those corners of make-believe where everything turns out just swell. A lot of stories, though, are taught under the aegis of an inside/outside metaphor that is never seriously questioned. The trope of the "outsider" is so widespread that it's hard to think of youth culture without its canonical misfits and outcasts. James Dean, Tom Sawyer and Huck Finn, Pippi Longstocking, Holden Caulfield, Eeyore, Greg Heffley from the *Diary of a Wimpy Kid* books, the flamboyantly gay high schooler in *When Everything Feels like the Movies*, Katniss Everdeen, and the anti-heroes in every Tim Burton film. But why feed kids this culture of virtuous rebellion—in institutionalized novels like *The Outsiders*—and, for the limited time they're young and in the cocoon of school, condition them to believe that the boorish world will allow them to be outsiders—march to the beat of their drummers, think outside the box, dare to be different, and so on—when for the most part it will allow for no such thing.

Which isn't so bad. Earlier this year the leader of a British Muslim organization defended "Jihadi John," the maniacal English ISIS holy warrior who was filmed slicing off the heads of some poor infidels, by saying, "When we treat people as if they are outsiders, they are going to feel like outsiders and they will look for belonging elsewhere." Asim Qureshi was probably right, though he shouldn't have said it, because ISIS executioners aren't the kinds of outsiders we should be romanticizing. Still, being a less dramatic outsider isn't much fun, either. Like if you're, say, an African or Syrian immigrant hiding out in a leaky boat bound for the Italian or Greek coasts or an unemployed Aboriginal woman living in an SRO in Vancouver's increasingly Soc-ish Eastside. It may be a pride-stiffening metaphor but it's a cosmic swindle to think that it's good, or cool and comfortable, being on the outside.

The metaphor—which is what we're using when we talk about an "outsider" without referring to a person physically removed from a structure that has a roof—is relatively new, going back only to 1907 when the figurative sense of "a person isolated from conventional society" first appeared. The origin of the English metaphor is telling because it points to a core issue: being an "outsider" is a fundamentally modern phenomenon that—like anomie, existentialism and nihilism—names the fundamentally modern condition of making your way in a world that has no grand narrative of moral purpose or an ethical centre. Most kids in Grade 8 might not understand this, and even if they could, it's not the message we'd want them to take away from their readings. Maybe they should enjoy the hallucination of goodness while they can because eventually they'll become jaded like everyone else. When I've taught *The Outsiders* in children's or YA lit class, I've always asked students if metaphorical "outsiders" could have existed in our mental horizons before the word existed, to which they always reply, yes, of course. But then even post-secondary readers and people who read only to escape can be forgiven their belief that words are referential pointers to things that exist in some unmediated real world that actually exists out there somewhere off the page. Ponyboy, who obviously doesn't exist as a real person but whose essay for his English teacher becomes the fiction we're reading as the novel we know as *The Outsiders*, would probably know that language can change how we act and think in the world for good or for bad intentions. He'd also probably know that having that knowledge, as unromantic and simple as it sounds, is probably the only way of being a genuine outsider.

About a decade ago I had a student in a novel class who also happened to have graduated from a UBC program I ran for low-income students in the Downtown Eastside many years before. Lex, a brash young woman with an attitude as sharp as her facial piercings, asked one day why her English teachers have always made students read stories about "fuck ups and dysfunctional people." I remember we were discussing *Platform*, the controversial novel for which author Michel Houellebecq was brought up on charges for inciting religious hatred against Muslims in France, but I don't remember what I said. Maybe I said that literature attracts people who don't have the inclination for law or plumbing but who want to contest the established order of things for some big social good, which part of me still thinks is true, or maybe I said that "fuck ups" are just more interesting to read about, which I'm sure has always been true. Tyler Durden, Clarissa Dalloway, Winston Smith, Meursault, Joseph K., Offred, Cayce Pollard—each is an outsider teetering at the precipice of some social or psychological marginality, and that teetering, which literary glossaries and professors call "conflict," is what puts the drama into a plot.

Lex's point, which was prompted by her belief that real marginalized people don't experience their marginality as romantic "outsiders," was that her liberal teachers childishly delude themselves into thinking that the system—the market economy, consumer capitalism or whatever—will come tumbling down if they can just keep on exercising critical thinking in the classroom, which is about as ridiculous as social-media hounds believing they're engaged in deep social change every time they click "like" or "share" or "reblog." There's nothing new about this. The liberal free market always recognizes the existence of rebels and dissidents—especially on Facebook and Tumblr, social networks that probably haven't entirely evolved beyond their adolescence—but, ultimately, conquers them with its strategies of containment. Still, I remember Lex's question because we happened to be talking about Houellebecq, a writer who has nothing good to say about liberals or academics and who's been called reactionary because he stands against the liberalization of values produced by the rebellious culture of the 1960s that became the neo-liberal corporate culture of the 1980s. A delightfully misanthropic heir to Albert Camus, the original "outsider" in the grand tradition of existentialist literature, who once said, "The texture of the world is painful, inadequate; unalterable, or so it seems to me," which doesn't sound too promising if you want to change the system or believe in "staying gold." And Houellebecq would agree, given that he's said, "We are now trapped in a world of kids. Old kids."

The metaphor of the outsider might be a childish liberal delusion, but then our world has witnessed what Joseph Heath and Andrew Potter, in *Rebel Sell*, call "the society-wide triumph of the logic of high school." And it runs much deeper than the spectacle of middle-aged guys skateboarding to work or the broader fascination with movies based on cartoon characters. Last year, *New York Times* film critic A.O. Scott argued that the concept of "adulthood" is dead. "The elevation of every individual's inarguable likes and dislikes over formal critical discourse," he said, "has made children of us all." I wouldn't argue with this, nor with his gorgeously judgmental admission of "feeling a twinge of disapproval when I see one of my peers clutching a volume of *Harry Potter* or *The Hunger Games.*" The judgment applies to adults, of course, not kids. I wouldn't give my thirteen-year-old acquaintance a copy of Camus's *The Outsider*, not because it would trigger an existentialist crisis in his head—I'm sure he's arrived at one on his own from all that online shooting he does—but because he probably can't, or shouldn't, fully understand its message, even though it's not too much different from the one he took from Hinton. When Meursault is standing on the beach with a gun in his hand—"staring at the sea, staring at the sand"— thinking about killing that Arab, "it crossed [his] mind that one might fire, or not fire—and it would come to absolutely the same thing." Ponyboy, after Johnny's death, calls his despair "too vast a problem to be just a personal thing" and then confronts it by calling his English teacher and writing the essay that we are reading as the novel; Camus shows us in Meursault that the struggle to find meaning where none exists is, though absurd, still absolutely necessary. There's nothing wrong with grown men riding skateboards or women wearing Hello Kitty barrettes, but adults, smart ones who read, understand that reading Camus, or Houellebecq for that matter, is like reading *The Outsiders* for grown-ups.

In January of 2015 the world was pulsating with all that cerebral talk of the right to free speech after those two "radicalized" Muslim guys—outsiders in their own way, I'm sure they'd call themselves—killed those twelve people at the Paris office of *Charlie Hebdo*. What many people don't know is that on that very same day a caricature drawing of Houellebecq appeared on the cover of the satirical magazine. It was a promotion for his new novel, *Submission*, also published January 7. The novel is a dystopian tale that imagines France governed by an Islamic government in the very near future, and for this reason it's tempting to point out here the seemingly absurd inversion of Meursault killing that Arab in Camus's novel, but there is no meaning in that. If there is some good in the outsider myth, whether a thirteen-year-old takes it from Hinton's adolescent book or you take it from grown-up novels, it's not in the myth itself; the good is that in reading these myths we get tools—an ability to read, follow a sentence from its subject to its verb through to its object and then to that mysterious end point where its grammatical signature generates meaning, string those meanings together to arrive at character and then plot and conflict, pause and dawdle a little at the metaphors that at first seem so baffling and therefore so irritating, and maybe cleave literal and figural meanings—that might just help us build meaning where no such meaning exists. And it never does, either in a novel or outside in the "real" world, does it? Not without the words that make that meaning happen. And this, like Ponyboy's essay that is *The Outsiders*, might just help us along the way.

My Avatar, My Self:
Are You for Real?

I looked at the Rorschach blot. I tried to pretend it looked like a
spreading tree, shadows pooled beneath it, but it didn't. It looked
more like a dead cat I once found. ... But even that is avoiding
the real horror. The horror is this: In the end, it is simply a
picture of empty meaningless blackness. We are alone.
There is nothing else.

—Alan Moore, Watchmen

In the fall of 2008, just as the world's ersatz run at economic prosperity was cascading into a recession, I had an epiphany. I was playing *Amped 2*, a snowboarding game, with my daughter on the family Xbox. I was racing along way behind her on the hill so I tried something risky on my side of the split screen—a multiple flip and 360°-spin combo—to gain points. I didn't expect it to work, and it didn't. All I remember is crashing into a railing, and then a short conversation.

Amused at my craptastic manoeuvring, my little girl tilts her head in my direction, but keeps her eyes on the screen and hands on her controller, and asks, "Oh, Pops, are you okay?" She wanted to know if my virtual crash—through some synaesthetic transubstantiation that unites avatar (the on-screen character one manipulates in video games) with flesh-and-blood player—had injured the real me. And with that one simple question my daughter melted everything solid—our game, the safe gap between fiction and reality, our selves—into air and in the process dragged one massive philosophical elephant into the room with us. I just wasn't sure if it was me or my avatar who noticed it come in.

"Yeah," I tell her, as my online self is repositioned at the top of the hill for the obligatory do-over, "I'm okay." Then, after a pause, "You *know* I'm not my avatar, right?"

I was trying to be clever in that patriarchal, father-knows-best way, but I was also genuinely concerned for my kid's metaphysical well-being. So between rail slides and grabs on our next run down the hill I rambled on about how her words had kind of just dislodged themselves—and us—from reality, and how maybe one day she'll probably read more books to figure out a thing or two about the real world that her question momentarily conflated with the fictional one on-screen.

People once believed, I told her, that the soul leaves the body at night when it sleeps, so what do you think happens to you, to your "self," when you're in a video game? What happens to you when, even in one of those entertainment situations that you're just not supposed to think about too much, you project yourself into a pixilated construct, into *Identity 2.0*, that near-mythical domain of a digital selfhood? Do you think it's like an out-of-body experience? I asked. Does you avatar change how you think and act in your physical life? Do you know that a study found that young people today can more easily identify cartoonish representations on-screen than animals and plants outside?

Yes, her question was only a juvenile Freudian slip that came from her naïve immersion in that Microsoft hyperreality console I bought for her. And yes, I'm sure I ruined our fun with my intellectualoid posturing, as I had many times before that evening. But I haven't forgotten that little rupture in the space-time continuum of our upstairs computer room, which also doubles as my office. It was a noodle scratcher, kind of like one of those high literary epiphanies you get in James Joyce, when "the soul of the most commonest object"—in this case, the family Xbox—jumped out at me faster than I could say *digitally mediated experience.*

If you spend hours staring at your Xbox—or PlayStation or Wii or whatever—your mind is going to walk headlong into a cosmic mash-up of fiction and reality. And no matter how savvy you think you are at not overstepping the metaphysical fault line that separates them, you just know there's going to be some impact on your psychic habits and practices, on how you think and see yourself and the world around you or on your screen. You don't have to be an old-fashioned Luddite or Marxist to understand that because a culture's mental habits are the products of its mode of production—how all its stuff is made—the suspension of disbelief we erect every time we're entertained by some fiction starts to unravel when those fictions are virtual. That's a stock part of our technological psychosis.

Theodor Adorno, a pop-culture critic who died long before Atari changed everything and gave the world *Pong,* said that with the birth of commercial mass media "the difference between culture and practical life disappears." He was thinking of TV, which can definitely play with your head but, unlike a computer screen, doesn't really talk back at you or give you that warm sense of community and connection. I can't imagine how he would wrap his mind around video-game culture. Lobbing quotes from dead German Marxists at young gamers who have only known a world dominated by personal media and advanced social media platforms like Facebook is like talking to the taxman about poetry. They might, like my daughter, offer a vacant stare and then blithely reassure you that yes, *they* understand the difference between reality and the fiction they are playing on-screen. And they probably do. My kid tells me this all the time. She *knows* she lives in a society geared towards image, what the postmodernists call the "society of the spectacle," and that she experiences simulated reality in the form of a fiction that sometimes seems more real than reality. She's even told me, with that *I can't believe you're so stupid* twinkle in her eye, that she's just a lot better at manoeuvring between virtual and non-virtual worlds than I am. And so she is.

It's enough to make the ground beneath me start feeling like molasses, but then for all the highfalutin abstractions and philosophical gems that come from technophiles warning about the dangers of gaming technology and from the cheerleaders of all things digital, of which there are so many more, there always seems to be a much simpler proposition at work: consumerism. All we're talking about is the conflation of the two old enemies— culture and economics—and about the fetishization of absolutist consumerism, the linchpins of the entire system.

Take the popular 3D online virtual-world game, *Second Life,* for example. It's a world, the homepage announces, "imagined and created by its residents." You create an avatar and then you do normal life things with it, like buy land, get married, mortgage a home, have an affair, open a small business. And so on— except that you can't die. The genius of SL, what makes it so much fun to "play," is that it offers a frighteningly beautiful—or beautifully frightening, I'm not sure which—vacation from your *self.* Like a 3D Facebook where the "walls" open up a fourth dimension and where "pokes" get more fleshy, this is technology that banks on luscious narcissism and the slightly psychotic need to have our every wish fulfilled.

Apart from the fact that they're so much fun, the genius of simulated-world games like *SL* is that they eliminate the difference between product and its ideology. You role-play your character in the fictional world, like I did with my *Amped 2* avatar, but that world isn't exactly fictional. Not quite. Making real money from your avatar's virtual endeavours is not only permitted; it's encouraged and expected. Like the notorious Anshe Chung, the *SL* avatar of the very real Ailin Graef, who was the first "resident" to make $1 million in her waking life from profits she earned selling—of all things—"real estate" in her second life on *SL*.

Featured on the cover of *Business Week* and hailed by CNN as the "Rockefeller of Second Life," the "out of character" Graef, who also goes by her "in character" name, now runs Anshe Chung Studios, a multimillion-dollar metaverse-development company that the World Economic Forum selected as "New Champion of the World Economy." It's entirely devoted to helping you, "as an individual organization or brand, to reincarnate and reinvent yourself in the Metaverse," so its website says.

Like a distilled galactic megamall with epic aspirations, *SL* is populated by six million avatars that represent, allegedly, millions of regular people around the world, but it's also home to first-life corporations and their real goods and services, which are sold to very real people for even more real money. Sony's there, Nike, too, and Toyota, American Apparel and even a Reuters news bureau. And so it goes—and grows, from real to fictional to virtual, with one fundamental component remaining consistent throughout: money. Eight or nine years ago, before the sub-prime mortgage meltdown in the nuts-and-bolts economy, a bank approached the director of advertising at video-game development giant EA and offered $1 million to sponsor virtual mortgages and loans for real estate in that other virtual-life-simulation game, *The Sims*. Curiouser and curiouser, as Alice cried out when she got unspeakably tall and cried her pool of tears in Lewis Carroll's novel, and certainly even more curiouser than that when we're talking about an Xbox game.

Virtual self-fashioning, whether in sporting games, dynamic first-person shooter games like *Grand Theft Auto*, or in the sophisticated simulated worlds like *SL* and *The Sims*, may be intellectually fascinating but they are just novel ways of making the "market," that boring and ugly old economic category that will never go away, appear young and sexy and not like a market at all but like a game or lifestyle. Maybe that's why most avatar templates—on *SL*, *The Sims*, *IMVU*—seem modelled on an animated aesthetic that always appears to resemble masturbatory pornography.

And sexed-up virtual selves is exactly where that fault line between the real and fictional or virtual gets impenetrably fuzzy. In a widely circulated 2008 news story a woman in the u.k. filed for divorce after she found her husband in real life cheating on her in his virtual one. His avatar was, presumably, in bed with someone else's avatar when his real wife walked into the room and witnessed the animated sex happening in the not-quite imaginary world of his computer screen. The year before, she'd caught him having sex with an online call girl, with the help of an online private detective. Stranger still is that the couple first met on *SL*. Their divorce hasn't been the only case of online infidelity.

It's all very puzzling, isn't it, negotiating this line between what's real and what's unreal? Look in the Gospel according to Matthew and you'll find Jesus saying, "I tell you that anyone who looks on a woman with lust has in his heart already committed adultery," which, if you take those things literally, means that pretty much everybody is guilty from the get-go. But guilt has always been more of an ideal, a sublime object of a moral ideology, rather than something real and palpable, especially in a digital age in which every temptation and vice has been monetized and put up for consumption. On the one hand, you forget the end of yourself and the beginning of your avatar when you slide between your in-world role and out-of-world character—your virtual represented self in the online game and your real flesh-and-blood self that is present in front of the monitor—but on the other hand, the fictional platform is built with an atomized and highly individualized consumer in mind. A deconstructed self that operates online and aims solely at the fetishization of its own demands—to do as it pleases—is a postmodern libertarian dream that at times appears more like a nightmare.

Which is why the avatar construction industry is not only about clothing and hairstyle, furnishings and commodities; avatars in role-playing games are generally without genitalia, although you can—through companies like SexGen Platinum and XCite Online—buy modifications that "attach" appropriate genitalia to the virtual self you chose as your avatar. At Xcite!, for example, you can buy the Cock Classic—featuring three stages of erection, orgasm and masturbation animations, and orgasm particle effects—or the X3 Clit—"Welcome to the new standard of female genitalia"—for your avatar, and in *SL* you can teleport directly to the company "kiosk" and buy your sex wares there.

I'd like to think that it's like the Promethean myth replayed online, and there's certainly something voluptuously epic about the selves we represent ourselves with in virtual life. Even the etymology of the word "avatar" is revealing here: Sanskrit in derivation, the word means "the descent of a deity to the earth in an incarnate form." A deity that says, much like God responds when Moses asks his name, *I am that I am*: I am an avatar, and the end of my self, my singular purpose, is the satisfaction of my desires, which are also the desires of the companies who populate the virtual world. I am a consumer, in other words.

Like most older-than-forty people for whom virtuality means two-dimensional cerebral geekery and avatar means a thin white paddle that moves vertically across a screen with the sole purpose of hitting the "ball" back to the other side of the screen, I can't yet think of these economic objects gussied up to look like cultural ones as social networks—even though I know that's exactly what they are. They seem little more than flirtatious marketing devices, aesthetically pleasing but rather tawdry mechanisms for pulling gobs of money and a modicum of identity from neurotic, over-heated adolescents and adolescent-minded adults. They're fun, no question about it, but fun in the mindless, stimulus-response way that shiny objects and round things might be "fun" for newborns and puppies.

The thing is, I *know* I'm wrong. I must be. Like the return of the repressed, video and online games have moved from the geek micro-civilization that sustained them during the final two decades of the last century into the mainstream, and they are explosive in popularity, influence and, most importantly, sales. At the end of 2008, the *Economist* reported that global expenditures on video-game hardware and software for that one year would reach $49.9 billion. By my calculations, domestic expenditures in my household alone—on Xbox, PlayStation, DS and DS Light, Archos, *Guitar Hero*, the shelves upon shelves of discs bought to shove inside these things, the modifications to online avatars, and of course the repeat purchases the manufactured obsolescence of the video-game economy demands of its consumers—amounts to about $5000 of that. To say nothing of the hours of time invested in playing.

This makes books, the oldest mass medium in the world, specifically novels—the one art form that's always been tied to individualism and built on an acute consciousness of selfhood—look like a constantly depressed market sector in comparison. Which it very well might become.

If you're well read or at least up-to-date with the world of "Literature," you're sort of expected to believe that images are deceptive prison-houses that can easily be used for the purpose of ideological mystification. "The fundamental movement of the literary mind," says the clever literary critic Paul de Man, "espouses the pattern of a demystifying consciousness." Part of what it demystifies is that stubborn mental habit of confusing literature with reality. Fiction is fiction and the world "out there" is just that: the world out there, which is where it stays. Literature is about things, of course, but it's first and foremost about expression. It's about descrambling and decoding our world in words, even though most good literature aims to make reading like falling into a fictional rabbit hole where the language doesn't matter as much as the world that the words apparently create.

But it's *words*—always harder to understand and much less fun to look at—that can deliver us from evil and make us more complete thinkers, not *images*, certainly not something like a sexy anime-inspired icon that we pretend to be on-screen. This old truism goes way back to Plato who, in an influential little parable about prisoners locked in a cave and forced to look at shadows on a wall, said that people are imprisoned by their inability to see beyond the apparent surface of things. We're easily seduced by images and always mistake them for "true" content, in other words, because we like to think that an image—a painting, photograph, movie, or YouTube video—can somehow restore the objects they represent to some empirical state where they are just there, present and authentic, full of themselves.

Of course they can't. That's why images are representations: they re-present that which is present only in a real world that is, no matter how hard we try to arrest it, fleeting. The best expression of this little moral that's not really a moral is from the film *The Matrix*, in the scene in which Laurence Fishburne's ever-cool Morpheus offers Neo, played by Keanu Reeves, those two pills. "You take the blue pill—the story ends, you wake up in your own bed and believe whatever you want to believe. You take the red pill—you stay in Wonderland and I show you how deep the rabbit-hole goes."

I once told my daughter, months after that incident on the snowboarding hill, that her uncertainty during my accident meant that Morpheus was right. For her, my real self became what he called "residual self-image." The mental projection of my digital self. I've also asked her, "What would *you* do if you were Neo?" She tells me that she'd take the red pill, too, but she assures me that people in her generation are quite capable of jumping from online to offline without thinking. "It's like there's no difference for us," she says.

I'd like to think that, if I were given Neo's choice, I'd also choose the red pill. I still believe in the demystifying force of literature, which is a knowledge of grammar and rhetoric, and how, combined, they create the edifice we call history and culture. The thing is, I'm almost certain that my daughter, who is far more literate than I was at her age but equally savvy navigating in her virtual worlds, wouldn't take either one. She would refuse on the grounds that the offer amounted to a false dichotomy, and tell Morpheus to take a hike, stop asking Neo such impossible questions, or at least ask him to rephrase the question in terms she understood.

Along the Brittle Treacherous Bright Streets of Memory

There is a memorable dialogue in *Total Recall*—Paul Verhoeven's 1990 film, not the 2012 reboot—where Kuato, the psychic resistance fighter who consists of a head and arms poking out of his brother's stomach, asks Douglas Quaid, the metaphysically baffled hero played by Arnold Schwarzenegger, what he wants. "The same as you; to remember," Quaid replies in that familiar Austrian brogue. "But why?" Kuato asks. "To be myself again." At which point Kuato says something that accents the otherwise kitschy pop sci-fi thriller with a dash of existential gravitas: "You are what you do. A man is defined by his actions, not his memory."

I remember only fragments of the film. Like, obviously, Sharon Stone and the three-breasted Martian woman ("Baby, you make me wish I had three hands!"), and I remember how Quaid shoots his wife in the head and delivers that smackdown line: "Consider that a divorce!" I watched it again recently because I was curious how it compares to the remake and if its message still resonates twenty years later, in the age of Facebook Timelines, Instagram and cloud computing. Heidegger, the whackadoodle philosopher whose work is as bewildering as the uncanny premise of *Total Recall*, said, "technology is a way of revealing," and lamented that it's "actions not words that count" in our technological world, and I wondered also how our understanding of memory might have changed, too.

When I saw the trailer I was sitting in a theatre with my daughter. I remember telling her I'd go to see it but that I was surprised they were doing another version. "It won't be as good," I said, invoking the definitive arrogance of my inner primordial father, although I did concede that re-rebranding the 1966 sci-fi classic—Philip K. Dick's underappreciated story "We Can Remember It for You Wholesale"—with Colin Farrell as the proletarian hero and Bryan Cranston of the former it-show *Breaking Bad* might popularize among younger people the topic of how memory is influenced by technology. She said she didn't even know there *was* another version, which, in one of those small epiphanies that punctuate the mundane business of parenting with some generational dramatics, left me disjointed. *"Seriously? You've never heard of the original? With Schwarzenegger? Really? Rilly?"*

Hyperbolic parental antagonism aimed at the perceived ignorance of younger people doesn't really deserve much attention, but it does demonstrate just how dialectical history, that incessant clash of memory and modernity, happens in our real-time conversations. Happy to inhabit the contradiction, she and I often exaggerate the generational theatrics that pit her youth against my age. She's spellbound by CGI animation; I say it's nothing more than a video-game-induced aesthetic form. She doesn't have a problem with Japanified youth culture; I think anyone older than twelve who models their hair after a fictional anime character looks absurd. Her friends wear low-rise skinny jeans, live most of their lives online and see Julian Assange as a revolutionary hero for their freedom of speech; I don't. When I recently told her about a Columbia University study that "proved" Google is having a negative effect on our capacity to remember things—it's becoming, a 2011 *Guardian* story reported, "a replacement for the ancient human faculty of memory"—she countered with her own logic. The conclusion, she said, must be wrong because relying on digital archives to remember things just shifts the energy we put into remembering acts, facts and experiences to other pursuits—presumably to other knowledge bytes that involve underused executions of the cerebral cortex, like looking at cat pictures and gifs on Tumblr.

Inside me I'm pretty sure there must be an old man sitting in a rocking chair on a porch, sporadically yelling at the kids playing in front of his house. He's waiting to become the person who's convinced himself that he's still a *young* man, biding his time and clutching his own memories, like Thor wields *Mjölnir*, to defend against becoming, ungracefully, a farcical geezer who is out of touch. In *Total Recall* Quaid grasps at memories because he wants to prove that he *is* actually a man named Quaid, not a knock-off named Hauser, an agent whose memory was erased and implanted with a new one. For my inner old man, memories are probably a purely defensive verbal strategy that I use against the silent immanence of my own increasing irrelevance and eventual mortality, getting louder and more stubborn as I gradually disengage from the youth of life.

I used to think that my girl was rather loopy because she has always been avowedly unhistorical in her thinking but remembers the most bizarre particulars of the past—the purple awning at the store on Nanaimo Street just north of Broadway that sells irises and little cedars, her Grade 5 teacher's eyes, the scent of our first dog's front paw. Sometimes it seemed to me that children, like animals and people who share their every waking thought and action on Twitter, live in a perpetual present: all that exists for them is the world as they see it in some hallucinated version of real-time that they do not understand is just as mediated as any other experience. The question is, how do we make sense of it all, remember it?

Years ago, standing at the corner of Penticton and Dundas in my East Vancouver neighbourhood, I was walking the dog with my daughter and I found myself explaining to her what I thought was good and bad about the kinds of memories we elect to remember, and I mentioned that when Dumbledore, that wonderful old wizard in *Harry Potter*, tells Harry, "It does not do to dwell on dreams and forget to live," he sounds an awful lot like Nietzsche. I've resurrected that memory so often it's become an epic, as if it were a conversation that singularly restructured my kid's mind forever. I've even sutured it in my head to the e.e. cummings poem about how a man's heart, "singing like / an idiot whispering like a drunken man," encounters his mind "along the brittle treacherous bright streets / of memory." It seems even more epic that way. My daughter remembers it, too, though it's likely that her head consigned it to the "shit my dad says" drawer, which is probably where it belongs.

Milan Kundera, in his cerebral novel *Identity*, challenges the cliché that older people are more inordinately drawn to memory than the young. It's a mathematical paradox. "Men grow old," he says, "the end draws near, each moment becomes more and more valuable, and there is no time to waste over recollections." So why remember anything when, in the finite economy of the time we have available to us, every minute you put to recalling the past is a minute that will not go to *having* an unmediated experience of the present? I don't know if I agree with his logic. I crave unmediated experiences in the present, like most people, but as I've aged, my memory of these experiences calcifies into nodes of nostalgia.

In Dick's story—and in both films—Douglas wants to be a secret agent and visit Mars but he can't afford the actual experience,
so he visits REKAL Inc., a company that implants "extra-factual"
memories. They're constructed but remembered as if they're
real. When he expresses doubts about the two fictional memories he's about to pay for, the salesman tells him, "You can't be
this; you can't actually do this. But you can *have been* and *have
done*." The verbal trick in tense is another way of saying that
memory, although we think of it as a blue recycling bin of facts—
dates, places and people locked into real history—capable of
being asserted in literal sentences, is far more metaphorical than
literal language. Memories can be *had* through language—and,
in the film at least, they can be implanted for a price, which
sounds like improbable sci-fi but is not too far removed from the
memory microchips a team of scientists in California have implanted in rats to demonstrate that synthetic memories can in
fact replace organic ones in the mind.

Plato, that curmudgeonly old Greek philosopher, makes a
point that's relevant here. He tells the story in *Phaedrus* about
Thoth, the Egyptian god of writing, who offers King Thamus
the gift of writing as a remedy to aid memory. Thamus doesn't
take the gift. Writing won't help memory or make people wise,
he says, but will just lead to more forgetfulness and artificial wisdom. Plato made the same argument against the Sophists, the
travelling professors of ancient Greece who taught public speaking, poetry and the "art of memory."

Conservative technophobe that he was, Plato thought our
reliance on writing was wrong because compared to "living memory"—which means capital P presence—writing is a synthetic
technology, a mnemotechnic, and it has the same relation to the

remembered event as a prosthesis to the limb it replaces or as a picture of you to you. His fear that knock-offs are worse than originals is kind of like the contemporary hipster neurosis about keeping appearance—facial hair, retro shirts, stomach paunches— more original than originality itself, or at least authentic enough, close enough to the original, so that it's not co-opted as fashion by corporate cool hunters. It's this fear of being pulled into the narrative of mainstream history that sustains that wonderfully revealing joke: *How did the hipster burn his tongue? He drank his coffee before it was cool.* The hipster doesn't want the coffee to be cool, no more than Plato wants writing to represent "living memory."

Versions of this same neurosis appear in *Total Recall* and Dick's other stories and their film adaptations. Think of replicant hunter Harrison Ford's confusion as to whether or not he is, in fact, a replicant himself in the cyberpunk classic *Blade Runner*, or Tom Cruise's worries over *precognition*—the noirish memories of history that has yet to happen—in *Minority Report*, or even Matt Damon's dread that free will is always already manipulated before it's executed as "free" or "will" in *The Adjustment Bureau*. My daughter adores the postmodern aesthetic in these films but doesn't think of them as warnings about the excesses of technology; they're just reminders, she thinks, that we can't renounce artifice and fiction any more than we can renounce reality itself. It could be that she's quite a Nietzschean that way.

But then so, too, is culture. The clash of memory and modernity, and the enthronement of obsessive-compulsive novelty that forgets real material history, is the cornerstone of postmodern capitalism. Which is why, in the marketplace, perversion and excess are no longer perverse or excessive. Think of artist Damien Hirst's maggots hatching in real-time or his shark pickled in formaldehyde and framed as art. Or, even more banally still, think of that novel *Fifty Shades of Grey*. At one point in history, novels about "kinky fuckery" would have been too odd for mass-market consumption, or their stories would be relegated to the ego-stroking corner of the blogosphere, but their radical new-ness, packaged with the euphemistic term "mommy porn" and legitimized by millions of regular suburban "soccer moms," in effect conquers its coolness and places it squarely into the main-stream of consumption. It's what Henry Ford meant, I think, by his well-known dictum "history is bunk" and what Schumpeter years later called "creative destruction" and business strategists call "planned obsolescence."

Forgetting is the new black, and it's been that way for a while. Against the ancient relationship between memory and creativ-ity—remember how the old Muses who inspired the arts are the daughters of Mnemosyne, Goddess of Memory?—it's the post-modern impulse to forget that sparks thought and imagination. And yes, "blessed are the forgetful," Nietzsche once said, "for they are done with their stupidities as well," a line repeated ver-batim at a crucial moment in the 2004 film *Eternal Sunshine of the Spotless Mind*, which like the Dick story involves a business that erases memories and fabricates new ones to suit consumer demand. Like the denials of death that define the narrative struc-ture of video games, Lacuna Incorporated promises the ability to erase the past, start over and aim for a better resolution.

Which brings us back to the premise of *Total Recall*. Memory, far from being the innate record of events that happened in some real past and filed in the hippocampus where they can be written and replayed, is manufactured and prosthetic, much more metaphorical than literal and in good part inspired by forgetting.

In a head scratcher of a passage, the French writer Baudelaire said that the beauty we take from writing—which is "the representation of the present"—is "due to the essential 'present-ness' of the present." Like memory, writing is not a factual reconstruction but an interpretive act that tries always to break out of language and resurrect the reality of a moment but is always bound to fail. Here the ancient Platonic idea is in line with a 2012 report by the British Psychological Society debunking the biggest myths about memory—among them, that memory literally works like a video recorder, or that some people have so-called "photographic memories," an impossibility that treats what can only ever be a verbal approximation of an empirical condition as an equation of empiricism itself.

From the sublime reaches of philosophy, literature and psychology to the ridiculousness of social networks, consider Facebook. What mechanism more than this, which we regularly complain about for its virtuality but then always go back to, illustrates that memory has more to do with fiction than it does with reality? Timeline was—and still is—marketed benignly as a narrative means to "tell your life story with a new kind of profile." What you see on the promotional video is the iconic image of a little boy held up by his father in a pool. Click play and you'll see and read about Andy Sparks, who was born in 1974, and, according to the marketers, his life up until this point has been unique and worthy of commemoration. Though it has the haunting aesthetic of an elegy, Andy's life as it is remembered and timelined portends only good things in the future, especially through the soundtrack, which is like a secular electro version of what a reasonably good person might hear when he's walking around Heaven. It's a spectacle staged to convince us—or Andy—that we live in a real world, just like in Dick's story "Time Out of Joint," where the hero—like Jim Carrey in *The Truman Show*—lives in a small town but discovers that this life is a constructed reality designed to keep him satisfied and keep him from knowing that he is *really* living in a future Earth.

At any rate, as a visual repository of memory that users control in real time, Facebook vindicates Freud's old argument that the human personality "is a work of art: a construction made by human beings with the means at their disposal...good, bad, incomplete, imperfect." Timeline—maybe all of Facebook—is just a marketing device intended to make users feel like they control the narrative presentation of their lives, but it's also a protective shield against the unbearable trauma of aging and death. It doesn't just give us our memories: as a corporate platform masquerading as a portal to our friends and interests, Timeline tells us how to remember and structures memories for us. It's ingenious, really, because it marks the perfect convergence of memory and modernity, and it enthrones marketing with the aura of authentic nostalgia. It is, just as Quaid describes his own emplottment in his story to Cohaagen, the vile Martian governor who's been manipulating the entire story in *Total Recall*, "the best mind-fuck yet."

Talking Dread: Zombie Sluts, Purple Cows and the Pornography of Death

If it exists, there is porn of it. No exceptions.

—Meme Rule 34 of the Internet

Even death? Is a corpse, whether decaying or theatrically reanimated as a zombie, arousing? Sure, sex and death are as intimately attached as any categorical facts of life we push into clashing contrasts, and the dichotomy separating a body's desires from its eventual expiration can be deconstructed faster than you can say "Freud." But then why would anybody want to personify this deconstruction? I've been wondering about this ever since an acquaintance of mine, a self-professed slut and aficionado of the dark arts whom I befriended during an erotic literature and marketing project, hooked up with the current little pop-cultural craze over zombies.

"I've never done this sort of thing before," Vee told me with ersatz apprehension, "but I'm going to an 'adult' Halloween party as a zombie slut. I didn't want to be the French maid or wanton librarian. Been there, done that, you know? I want to go deeper."

"That's quite the dialectical image," I said to her. I had neither been there nor done that, and as a rule I don't get invited to parties where women are outfitted with ball gags and leather-bound men wear leather codpieces. Nor did I know what she meant by going deeper, though I imagine there was just as much a metaphysical thrust in those words as a physical one. And I'm still not sure why any person—except maybe a troubled attention seeker or grim aesthete—would even want to dress up as a zombie slut.

I eventually asked Vee why she chose to dress in an ensemble of culturally acceptable tastelessness and what this choice of hers might say about her pleasure-seeking subculture that, at least this year, fetishizes the walking dead to the point that even this icon, in its catatonic persistence, gets co-opted into the broader cultural treadmill of marketable pornography.

She thought my question was a bit of a cerebral downer. It was only a Halloween costume, after all, and she was simply engaging in some "bawdy theatrics" for the purpose of her "ongoing dramatic carnality." Which wasn't that surprising to hear, because in one of her other guises, she plays a run-of-the-mill forty-something sex blogger who writes tales about how she managed to avoid a head-on collision with her midlife crisis by becoming a serial adulterer.

"Sex and death," like the poet Yeats once said, "are the only things that can interest a serious mind." Maybe so. I admit that I found Vee more intelligent than the average online scribbler in the tawdry depths of the sex net, where "hacks" are as common as pop-ups, but perhaps this was because, to most people, vitality and mortality are undeniably bracing, and ostensibly philosophically "deep" bedfellows.

The ancient Greeks believed sex involved a violent expenditure of the body's resources. An orgasm—in men, they meant, insensitive sexists that they were—involves the involuntary paroxysm of ejaculation, wherein a guy lays out both his reason and sperm. Plato, for example, once said that in moments of sexual pleasure a man "pants in strange ways, and is driven completely out of his senses...dying with enjoyment."

Sex, for Plato, marks the point at which life begins and begins to end. Like the first bookend on a shelf, sex is all good and fine and functional but it leads to procreation, the closest we can ever come to immortality, which is of course what we all crave, and then eventually gives way to the last bookend, which is death. Animals "fall prey to a violent love-sickness," Plato says, and they are "ready to die" for it, and the same goes for the human animal, too. Every person, he says in *The Laws*, "desires to become famous and not to lie nameless after he has died."

Vee had a lot to say about the convergence of sex and death in popular culture, and though every once in a while she sounded remarkable for all that metaphysical rhetoric with which she laced her ribaldry, much of what she told me seemed to be advertising copy for her own personal brand. It was a specialty of hers, thematically related to her official daytime persona—which was more real than symbolic—as owner of an adult boutique somewhere in Utah. She spoke of zombie porn and listed masturbatory fodder—like *Night of the Giving Head* and *Porn of the Dead*—but she also knew the more mainstream works like *Night of the Living Dead* and *Shaun of the Dead*, and she knew of the *Walking Dead* TV series and the Brad Pitt film *World War Z*. But it was promotional, not philosophical.

Though she did ask, somewhere in her response to my first question, if I had read Seth Grahame-Smith's bestselling mash-up, *Pride and Prejudice and Zombies*—yes, I'd seen it—and if I noticed how the sexual tension mixed in with the zombie theme.

She recited almost verbatim a passage I either didn't notice or just didn't pay attention to when I looked at it. Elizabeth, having just given the notorious zombie slayer his gun, extends her hand and says, "Your balls, Mr. Darcy?", at which point he closes her hand around them and says, "They belong to you, Miss Bennet." They were talking about bullets, of course, but still, "Upon this, their colour changed, and they were forced to look away from one another, lest they laugh." That little innuendo, as I understood the intricacies of Vee's mind, vindicated the fusion of sex and death in entertainment culture today.

Like Grahame-Smith's sort-of-funny derivative book, there's an earnest superficiality about zombie culture, but that superficiality sits on top of an embedded economic logic. Vee liked her zombies because they were popular and novelty was her thing. Plus, they made for good porn. They're undead, yes, but more sinister than that, at their putrid core they're kind of like an unsophisticated brand for everything. Doesn't the simple fact of the zombie's visual distinction, apart from the requisite fear and horror it intends to elicit, explain the current trend? They are visually remarkable, or what marketers call "purple cows": products that draw attention to themselves and, on the basis of superficial appearance alone, as compared to any point of content in itself, create the illusion of being different from all other products in a similar market. Like a rhetorical trope, the popularity of zombies marks the return to some niche state of childhood make-believe fantasy of pure originality.

The BC government put out a "Zombie Preparedness Week" public service announcement in 2012. It looked like it was preparing us for a zombie invasion but it intended only that we take seriously the government's "be prepared" mantra. "While the chance of zombies a-knockin' on your door is pretty slim, we do believe that if you're ready for zombies, you're ready for any disaster." It was theatricality underwritten by social media deployed for the purpose of persuading the public to prepare for earthquakes and tsunamis.

That campaign was built on the success of the fictionalized public service announcement undertaken in the u.s. in 2011, where the Centre for Disease Control—which itself plays a prominent role in the first season of *The Walking Dead*—issued a Zombie Apocalypse public service announcement video. When the CDC put out that viral video, its servers crashed. It was as if, momentarily, civic society took the form of a video game, and the only way to reach the public was to act out the fantasy in character.

Axe, Doritos, Honda, Geico—they've all enlisted the remarkable visual appeal of zombies to repackage their products as novelties. In a particularly bizarre case of zombie marketing, Sears framed its Craftsman line of chainsaws under the banner "Craftsman vs. Zombies." Likewise, the Ruger Corporation, an American manufacturer of the sort of guns that cause so much real fear and anxiety, stamped its LCP380 pistol with the video-game tag "The Zombie Slayer," embossed in a casual font along the barrel. This comes after a series of other zombiefied marketing stunts involving other weapons, notably a product called Zombie Max ammunition, which promises to "put the dead to rest for good" but which also comes with this psychotic disclaimer: "Zombie Max ammunition is not a toy. It is intended only to be used on zombies, also known as the living dead, undead, etc. No human being, plant, animal, vegetable or mineral should ever be shot with Zombie Max."

The most significant zombie-marketing moment recently was the release in November of *Black Ops II: Zombies*, the ninth game in the *Call of Duty* franchise of first-person shooters. The game, which offers wonderful characterizations of real historical figures—Fidel Castro, for example, that still-living representative of apparently dead Marxism, and George Romero, the famed zombie-film director—and curious plot lines but which is really not too different from any other weapon-based game, made more than $500 million in twenty-four hours of sales and apparently became the biggest entertainment launch of all time.

In a way, as the designated it-character type of so much popular entertainment culture this year, from film to novels to advertising, zombies are exemplary economic icons of a kind of childish consumerist fetishism built entirely on symbolism. Zombies are infantile or rudimentary desire, pure and simple, but they masquerade the movements of market-driven capitalism. They are, to use an analogy from Chris Harman's 2009 book *Zombie Capitalism*, iconic totems used to reanimate the consumption of products by appealing to a childlike desire for radical newness. Even after it's been ground through marketing filters, nothing is ever enough for desire: there's still the empty robotic movement of consumption.

But their association with the pornography of excessive violence shouldn't be underestimated. There's a dialogue in Cronenberg's historical film *A Dangerous Method* in which Freud—played by Viggo Mortensen—admits to his colleague—Sabina Spielrein, played by Keira Knightley—that her research has changed his view on the primacy of the sex instinct. "I suppose," Freud says, referring to "Destruction as the Cause of Coming into Being," a paper in which Spielrein argued that the sex drive is a demonic and destructive force, "there must be some kind of indissoluble link between sex and death." The real Freud went on to argue that all of our behaviour comes down to these opposite drives. We instinctually desire sex to please and perpetuate ourselves, and we're pushed to self-destruction to return our organic bodies back to an inanimate state. No, he didn't say anything about a third impulse that makes dead bodies reanimate and walk around looking for flesh or brains to consume—depending on which zombie myth you follow.

People have made all sorts of wild speculations about what the zombie *really* means in the bigger symbolic field. It's the robotic impulse to consume, it's the individual living under the apocalyptic threat of viruses and pandemics, it's the melding of both male and female sexual organs in some unholy postmodern union that defies nature—the one rigidly looking to satisfy its singular desire, and the other about to devour it—and in the process give a new birth. The one I find most convincing comes from Slavoj Žižek, the Slovenian writer who's been hailed and harangued as "the Borat of philosophy." He calls the zombie the "figure of pure habit." "At the most elementary level of human identity, we are all zombies." Similar to Freud, who was always going on about the tendencies we repress to appear civilized, scratch the symbolic veneer from the person, Žižek says, and you'll find zombies, "the disavowed foundation of our own humanity." The zombie is the resounding reminder of the most elemental human—who eats and pisses and fucks and gives birth—in all its pullulating glory. Transferred to a broader social context, this may be another way of saying that there is something fundamentally gross about the recurring movement back to the elemental fact of our ugly existence. Zombies, apart from functioning as novel re-brandings of the same-old products and as a wider motif for understanding the way the liberal market-place constantly brings itself back to life, may also be just the proverbial skull in the corner of the room reminding us that we are going to die.

None of this is what Vee had in mind when she told me that her choice to go to that party dressed as a zombie slut was because she wanted to "go deeper." My first impression of her was that she was an egotistical hedonist, which can serve as a temporary antidote to our consciousness of our own mortality, but there was something else there. "I have a very dark side," she explained when I asked if the zombie component of her costume wasn't her just capitalizing on what happened to be a popular motif. "No. I'm drawn to any and many things related to death. Cemeteries, csi shows, torture, caskets, All Saints' Day, the archangel Azrael." I couldn't help but think Vee's fascination with death was like Marx's argument that capital is "dead labour, which, vampire-like, lives only by sucking living labour, and lives the more, the more labour it sucks."

Eventually, Vee wrote me a vivid summary of the Halloween party, and her narrative was far more indebted to the predictable cadence of pornography than to the cryptic rhythms of an obituary or zombie film, but it wasn't without its otherworldly undercurrents. "At the party, my Daddy took me to the big wooden cross. He helped me take off my clothes. I was leaning forward against the cold, polished wood of the cross, wearing nothing but my platform shoes." And so on the story went, complete with flogging and the administration of torture. Using the spectacle of crucifixion to get to some sexual end point puts a new spin on "la petite mort," but she told me earlier that she often communicated with martyred saints. Yes, the dead ones. "And I've gotten answers," she assured me, though I don't imagine playing the part of a zombie whose wrists and ankles are tied to a St. Andrew's Cross while being sexually tortured was one of them, but I may be wrong.

At first I thought Vee's entire persona—the libertarian feminist sex blogger, the gothic lover of the macabre, the submissive, the adult-store entrepreneur—was just an eloquent finish on what was an exuberantly libidinous set of desires. In one of our last exchanges, she suggested, in response to something I said about her being publically flogged on that cross, that she probably found offensive, "Maybe we need a little bit of death every now and then."

The Revolution Will Not Be Televised—But It Might Be Carnivalized 'n Shit

I saw The Hunger Games today... it was very inspiring. It felt like
almost a mimic of my exact life and shit. I know it. I was like, "Baby
we gotta be on that movie board when they writing this shit."
And I saw Lenny Kravitz ... and shit.

— KANYE WEST

I went to see the second *Hunger Games* film, too. I wouldn't say it was a "mimic of my exact life and shit," and I didn't tell the babe I went with that we should be on board "when they writing this shit" because I haven't got a clue what that even means, though Kim Kardashian might. Still, like Kanye, *Catching Fire* did inspire me. It got me wondering about the culture industry and revolution and shit. Can a revolutionary idea go on without a celebrity to endorse it? Does a radical thought—like the one at the core of Suzanne Collins's popular young-adult novels and the film franchise about that untwerkable Katniss Everdeen valiantly challenging the cinematically sexy propaganda machine that holds a totalitarian state together—have any substance, does it have any *meaning* at all, if it's not framed by a blinged-out telematic culture built on a ramped-up consumer fetish for camera-ready fashion and stylized cosmetic trinketry?

Maybe it can, maybe it can't or maybe it never could. The day before we went to see *Catching Fire* my mate and I considered going to an IMAX. We were stoked because someone in the *Wall Street Journal* said Katniss Everdeen's glitzed-up entrance into the gladiatorial arena before the Quarter Quell contest—that supercharged death match in which kids kill other kids on reality TV for the viewing pleasure of the citizens of the Capitol and as a reminder to the impoverished people of the outlying districts that they shouldn't even think about rebellion—was visually unprecedented in the IMAX "theatre geometry." That format made Jennifer Lawrence's Katniss, whose costume and eye makeup made her look like Elizabeth Taylor's twenty-four-karat-gold–capped Cleopatra in that 1963 blockbuster film, a work of visual art you'd want to see for its own sake. But going to see a movie that challenges our fascination with eye-stroking superficialities that conceal entirely repulsive social practices at a venue that celebrates visual enhancement is hypocritical, unless you're an unflappable hipster who thinks your day-to-day hypocrisies are just you being ironic. But then who knows? In one of those interminable bytes of intellectual history, Machiavelli, the original gangsta of political philosophy, once said "the masses are always impressed by the superficial appearance of things." Though the world looks prettier when I push that thought away, I'm sure he's probably right. Maybe, like small children and kittens, and for sure like the telematic citizens of the Capitol driven by a manufactured desire to look spectacular and to look at people and things *as* spectacles, we're more motivated by polished shiny objects and round things than by any ethical principles.

In any case, we went to see *Catching Fire* at a more plebeian cinema. My mate has read all the novels—and made me a fan of

the badass heroine—and she'd talked about their political allusions and allegorical significance with such unbridled enthusiasm
that we thought staying away from the pomp of IMAX was the
good and right thing to do. Plus, it was the week of Black Friday,
and we'd gotten so chaffed at the hyped state of consumer culture on Facebook and TV that we were just down with all that
radically democratic talk that, at least momentarily, accompanied
the film's release.

But something strange happened while we were sitting in our
chairs, chowing on popcorn and waiting to be enlivened with
that hopeful revolutionary promise with which the first film
ended. In the anticipatory half-lit communal haze when the
audience, lulled into a fantasy sense of our own good fortune,
was watching trailers and aestheticized commodities appear on-
screen like metaphysical totems of a devoutly narcissistic society
of the spectacle—just like the one emplotted in the film—there
was an ad for the *Catching Fire* collection by CoverGirl. To most
normal people, trailers aren't that important, and they weren't
for us, either—at least not at the time. When you're sitting in the
theatre and the images appear, like the shadows presented to the
prisoners in Plato's cave, all that you really want to do is sort of
half watch them through to the feature presentation. But with
that thirty-three-second spot squeezed innocuously between the
last trailer and the first shot—when we see Katniss in an
Appalachian forest ready to fire at wild game to provide food for
her family—ideology came down on us like an iron fist encased
in a gossamer glove.

The Capitol Collection, named after the capital city of post-
apocalyptic Panem—the self-contained dystopian metropolis set
against the West Coast mountains—is a display of brute power

framed in a half-minute carnivalesque ad. It's a line of makeup personified by characters "inspired" by the novels but clearly more indebted to the capital revenue—some $700 million—generated by the first film in the series. "Something hot is coming to the Capitol," the script on-screen reads, followed by the parallel slogan "12 Districts, 12 Hot Capitol Looks" and punctuated with that iconic blazing jaybird, the franchise's revolutionary brand and CoverGirl's cosmetic brand makeover. The ad anticipates the costume and design of the film, an affably insane mash-up of the decadence of Imperial Rome and a postmodern feudal cast that could have been inspired by a Dr. Seuss film, heavily accented with the proto-fascist cleanliness of 1930s' Germany and the scandalously self-absorbed techno-couture of our own world. Most disturbing of all is that in what must be one of the most repulsively beautified divisions of labour in economic history, each "look" is CoverGirl's personification of the raw material, manufactured good or service that each district produces for the Capitol in the fictional world of the story. This economic organization is a nod to the "division of labour" of Adam Smith, the godfather of free-market capitalism who explained back in his 1776 book *The Wealth of Nations* that the greatest improvements in the productive power of labour lies in its separation into smaller, specialized tasks, "which occasions, in a well-governed society, that universal opulence which extends itself to the lowest ranks of the people."

District 1 represents the Capitol itself, where people don't really "do" anything except consume objects of conspicuous consumption. The CoverGirl marketers represent it with a woman in moribund gold whose decadent hair is reminiscent of either the extravagant wired headdresses of pre-revolutionary France or an Oompa Loompa. According to the advertising geniuses who provided rationalizations for each characterization on the website, this Capitol woman signifies "Luxury." District 2, responsible for masonry, is a minimally made-up meat and potatoes labour-inspired woman, and District 3, technology, is a sleek—and predictably Asian—woman with triangular eyebrows and futuristic headgear. The representative for livestock-producing District 10 is earth-toned, with something that looks like a Thanksgiving door ornament on her head, and the one from District 12, as you'd know if you've read the novels or seen the films, is stylized and coloured in hues reminiscent of mining. And so goes CoverGirl's cosmetic division of labour.

From the fetishistic luxury objects to the material ones, there's a perfect structural allegory here in how the Capitol celebrates the process of surplus-value extraction that defines its political relationship with the impoverished outlying districts. All the representative women are attractive and sexy, of course, but just like the commodities their Districts produce, they're all bound to function as spectacles for the Capitol and so bound by its spectacular economy of "opulence," to use Adam Smith's word, "which extends itself to the lowest ranks of the people." So before the film even begins, our attention is transferred from the anticipated political struggle—Will Katniss lead the revolution? How will it start? And the other questions with which the first film closed—to questions about what clothes to wear and what makeup to put on.

They say you're not supposed to shout "fire" in a crowded theatre if there's no real fire, but can you shout it when you spot an infernal ideological ploy at work? Theodor Adorno, the critic who was one of the first thinkers to write about the effects of film, TV and horoscopes on the popular mind, said that ideology comes to us in the form of contradictions. He said that to "manipulate the masses," the ideology of the culture industry must be "as internally antagonistic as the very society which it aims to control." The word "manipulation" is abrasive to people who've managed to hallucinate that each of their ideas have been manufactured in the pristine clarity of a mind centred in its own centredness and free of most external influence, but you've got to wonder what the Capitol Collection ad, presented a half minute before a film about a nascent rebellion against the Capitol in a theatre packed with young women, was aiming to do if not manipulate them with this contradiction. Ideology, it seems, happens in the quietest of moments, like during those thirty-three seconds in which we saw a glimpse of the parasitic betrayer of the film's intended message. Revolt against a society of the spectacle by becoming a spectacle yourself. The semiotician Roland Barthes, who looked at everything from pasta ads to TV sports as a system of signs that needs to be relentlessly decoded for the layers of meaning that conceal political principles to become intelligible, once said that a "healthy" sign is one that draws attention to its own arbitrariness and doesn't try to look "natural." By this logic, there's a playfulness in CoverGirl's District "looks," a kind of carnivalesque attitude wherein those who would aspire to the Capitol's ostentation do so with a sense of self-awareness or—shudder—irony, but even that sense of playfulness doesn't erase the clear-cut idea that these products are part of the very problem that the rebellion in the film is trying to challenge.

When CoverGirl announced its first-ever movie sponsorship—with this *Hunger Games* film—in May 2013, the popularity of the second instalment in the franchise was already geared more to the inoffensive costumes than to the political content of Collins's stories. "We wanted to redefine cosmetics' relationship to film in a fantasy-meets-reality beauty experience," said one VP at global P&G Cosmetics, CoverGirl's parent company. The campaign, she went on to say in language that was at once pretty and nebulous, "will bring beauty transformation to life in an aspirational, dramatic fashion." For its part, the production and distribution giant Lionsgate Films offered a more directly sinister position through one of its VPs. "The exquisite beauty and style in the world of the Capitol is a focal point of this film. Partnering with an innovative brand like CoverGirl to create an additional layer of beauty storytelling and inspiration for the fans is new territory that we're delighted to explore."

Not that it is surprising—though perhaps it should be—that the point in the Capitol Collection ad is not to make young women into politicized citizens ready to speak up against unfairness, let alone fire arrows at injustice, which I think is pretty close to the point of the original novels, but to secure their positions as consumer-actors who aspire to the Capitol, which just might be, as the VP reminds us, "a focal point of this film." Back in 1936, a time of economic injustice that was morphing into totalitarianism not entirely unlike the dystopian world envisioned in Collins's novels, Walter Benjamin invented the phrase "aestheticization of politics" to describe how fascism makes its politics look aesthetically pleasing. That's exactly what we saw happen in the theatre before the movie started.

I don't know how the other people in the theatre—especially the young women—read the ad, or whether they simply looked at it. There was one mildly irritating teenage girl sitting beside us whose phone kept glowing during the trailers, and I'm sure she probably wasn't paying too much attention. But then even if they weren't paying close attention, or even if they were and got drawn in by the theatrics, I find it hard to imagine that any viewer wouldn't be put off by CoverGirl's reinterpretation of the film's obscene political economy as thirty-three seconds of aestheticized drama. A few months before the movie came out Miley Cyrus was going around sticking her tongue out and taking off her clothes in response to the outcry she'd started over that twerking business, and in the midst of the heated argument over slut shaming and what young women should and shouldn't do in front of cameras, journalist Laurie Penny pointed out that "society does not care about young women…it cares about Young Women™ as concept and commodity." That seems to be the signal in that CoverGirl spot.

My daughter, for reasons that I still don't fully understand, won't see *The Hunger Games*, because she says all that rebellion is just so much politicized chatter, credible sounding window dressing that draws the smarter-than-*Twilight* set of young women fans into the theatre but establishes pretty much the same fascination with the culture of image consciousness that the novels contest. She likes the novels, but can't tolerate the very idea of watching this particular film on-screen, and she may have a point. More than twenty years ago, the old-school feminist Naomi Wolf, in that old feminist tome *The Beauty Myth*, which came out years before *Sex and the City* normalized the idea that a sexualized aesthetic is always a good and liberating thing for women to embrace, argued that "the beauty myth is always actually prescribing behaviour and not appearance." Appearance, though it seems superficial, can alter behaviour.

CoverGirl's cosmic reinterpretation of *The Hunger Games*, a story about affluent people taking pleasure in watching poor young people kill each other on TV, as a narrative of complicity with the Capitol and acquiescence to its garish spectacles in the name of fun, is certainly ballsy for its apparent reversal of original plot, but then cosmetics are in the business of making original things look different, aren't they? Marx has that great line about how history happens twice—the first time as tragedy, the second time as farce—and that seems exactly to be what happened here.

And yet style, whether in the colours a young woman puts on her eyes and nails or the types of sentences a middle-aged guy uses or a dramatically reactionary ad screened just before a politically radical movie, must matter to us, just as it matters in the universe of *Catching Fire*, where Katniss gradually starts to understand that her appearance is the key to her survival in the games because the TV audience will only take notice of her if she is beautified and made to look gorgeous by her "stylist," Cinna, played by the inordinately cool Lenny Kravitz, a figure who is killed off early in the movie for having styled a too-rebellious fashion statement. It's also the key to the entire revolution, which in the novels and films has a lot more to do with the semiotic simulations of clothing and accoutrements than we probably like to admit. The figure is heroic, in other words, because she has the appearance of a revolutionary and has learned how to play the cosmetic system of the games themselves, and in that respect maybe CoverGirl, despite its creepy politics, was on to something important because nobody ever said that pretty things and revolutionary spirit can't go together. My mate guffawed and chortled as much as I did during those thirty-three seconds, even though she's a stylish woman who happens to like makeup and probably owns some CoverGirl products. Even Emma Goldman, that old anarchist, vindicated beauty in the otherwise dour, firebrand context of political agitation. When she was publicly reprimanded by some earnest young zealot who allegedly told her that "frivolity would only hurt the cause" when he saw her partying, she responded by saying, "I want freedom, the right to self-expression, everybody's right to beautiful, radiant things." That exchange was the legendary source of that delightfully smartass feminist and socialist riposte: "If I can't dance, I don't want to be a part of your revolution."

I remember Don Draper saying in the first-ever episode of *Mad Men*, back when its writers seemed more interested in the rhetorical seductions of the advertising industry than the sexual seductions of secretaries, that "advertising is based on one thing: happiness," and then going on to tell some cigarette executive that happiness is "a billboard on the side of the road that screams with reassurance that whatever you're doing is OK. You are OK." That episode—"Smoke Gets in Your Eyes"—featured a sly nod to the work of the marketing and public relations philosopher Edward Bernays. The nephew of Sigmund Freud, he was the man who, beginning in the 1920s, applied psychoanalytical principles to marketing for American companies and, later, for the u.s. government in its ideological war against Germany and then the Soviet Union. In his most important work, *Propaganda*, a book published in 1928, when people talked more openly about how to use language to get people to desire products and then buy them in a free-market economy, he said, "The conscious and intelligent manipulation of the organized habits and opinions of the masses is an important element in democratic society. ... We are governed, our minds are molded, our tastes formed, our ideas suggested, largely by men we have never heard of. This is a logical result of the way in which our democratic society is organized. ... In almost every act of our daily lives...we are dominated by the relatively small number of persons...who understand the mental processes and social patterns of the masses. It is they who pull the wires which control the public mind." What this means—and what most of us who live in democracies are loathe to admit—is that we aren't as free as we like to think.

The menacing and affable leader of Panem reminds me of Bernays, especially in his understanding of propaganda. At one point President Snow—who's played by the downy-haired Donald Sutherland—and Katniss get together in one of the most important parts of the story to talk about—wait for it—the political implications of her dress. This part of the story is thicker in the novel's narrative. "'I didn't mean to start any uprisings,' I tell him," Katniss says. "'I believe you. It doesn't matter. Your stylist turned out to be prophetic in his wardrobe choice...you have provided a spark that, left unattended, may grow to an inferno that destroys Panem,' he says." Snow knows that it's appearances that matter more than intentions, not only for the luxuriants of the Capitol but also for the disaffected masses in the Districts. As for Katniss, well, she didn't want to inspire a rebellion, but that's what she ended up doing, partly as a consequence of her stylist—the same guy Kanye was going on about in that diatribe. Later in the novel, when Katniss is being beaten by a "Peacekeeper," her handler, Haymitch, intervenes. "'Oh, excellent.' His hand locks under my chin, lifting it. 'She's got a photo shoot next week modeling wedding dresses. What am I supposed to tell her stylist?'" The point here is that it doesn't matter if she deserves the beating or not. What matters, singularly, is her appearance at the photo shoot. Her life depends on how she appears for the cameras, as might the revolution.

Though the story is indebted to the Greek myth of Theseus and to the Roman concept of *panem et circenses*—the satirist Juvenal's term for "Bread and Circuses," the policy of shutting down dissent by giving people entertainment and food—Collins says she dreamed up the novels when she was flipping her TV between a reality TV show and war coverage from the Middle East. The trilogy is about, in essence, what it's like to live in a world where people "live" through their various virtual representations of themselves, a carnivalesque world that no longer discriminates between real-time war and hyperreal entertainment. Two years ago the *Economist* printed a review of the first *Hunger Games* and pointed out the ethical conundrum that must fester and sit uncomfortably in any thoughtful person who sees the film, except maybe Kanye. "How can such a film divorce the thrills it delivers from the fictional thrill-making that it has to deplore?" In other words, if it's a critique of visual culture, which it is, then how come it's a film? Lobbing around words like "contradiction" or "antagonism" doesn't really address this melon scratcher of a question, though it does ruin the "fun" of watching *The Hunger Games* as pure entertainment. Perhaps the best answer comes from the first film and novel when one of the characters, Gale, who by the end of the second installment is a declared revolutionary, asks, "What if everyone just stopped watching?" But even that's not much of an answer, is it?

F You, Professor: Tumblr, Triggers and the Allergies of Reading

I was having a coffee and reading a book when this kid who happened to walk by close enough to see the cover felt compelled to say the title out loud. "Allergies of reading," he said, and I looked up and saw he was beaming, pleased with himself for having breached the linguistic universe of grown-ups yet oblivious to the fact that he had misread the keyword in the title.

Not that it mattered. Phone in one hand and laptop in the other, earbuds plugged into his head, and the unctuous spackle of too many hours spent in front of a computer screen sparkling on his face, he just didn't look like he'd seen the inside of a book lately. I know. Times, and the way we "read," have changed. This was a "digital native," and his Internet culture is, as Jon Stewart once said, "just a world passing around notes in a classroom." Nor did the wired little snot-flicker's horizon of knowledge expand one bit when, doing my best finger-wagging pedant, I gave him the stink eye and corrected him. "*A – leh – go – reez*." His misreading was harmless, but it stayed with me, lodged in my brain like a parasitic leitmotif for the shoddy—and shitty—reading and writing habits that lead to nasty writing and hysterical misinterpretations of things.

Words define our virtual landscape, same as they did before screens, yet on most days "reading" them—from licence agreements to texts, posts, tweets, blogs and reblogs and all the other

stuff made of words and sentences that come before our eyes—
is something we do without thinking about what it means to
read. At that one "magical instant" in your childhood, the words
you were looking at, "that string of confused, alien ciphers," as
Alberto Manguel beautifully describes it in *A History of Reading*,
"shivered into meaning." In most cases, though, after that point,
the verb *read* is only a means to an end. We look at letters, de-
scramble words, more or less process them into syntactic units,
hope for the best when we factor in the regulatory punctuation,
and then, like the computations in a math equation that become
transparent once we've figured out the answer, we arrive at the
meaning without giving much thought to the process that
brought us there.

Linguists and literary theorists like to say that anything that involves language—road signs to laws, novels to sexts—happens as
though, in effect, language doesn't really exist, which sounds
about right to me. "The greatest trick the Devil ever pulled," I tell
my students—none of whom are old enough to remember that
I'm pirating a line from Verbal in *The Usual Suspects*—"was convincing the world he didn't exist," and the same can be said for
language, both the reading and writing parts. As the philosopher
Merleau-Ponty once said, "The perfection of language lies in its
capacity to pass unnoticed." That's a good thing to know, I tell
them, when you're reading, say, the instructions for your IKEA
furniture, a syllabus, a status update or cultural flotsam on Dis-
tractify.com. But when you study in the prison-house of school,
you're forced to *read* words and sentences that you might not like
or, if you do like them, you can't click "like" and then move on,
gnat-like, to the next language thing on your screen; nope, you've
got to slow down the reading and attend to the—*eek!*—grammar

and rhetoric, which are the twin pillars of our cultural DNA, the elemental things that make thinking happen and hold civilization together in that loud superstructure of linguistic communication.

A recent University of Washington study of digital books found that about 25 percent of students still bought print versions of e-texts they received for free, and e-reader sales are slumping, apparently, but it seems clear to me that dead-tree book literacy has taken a pretty big hit in the last decade or two. Late in 2014, StatCan reported that more than 25 percent of university grads in the country have a literacy score at the second level or lower on a five-tier system. Lower scores in the survey "indicate that individuals may be less likely to be able to integrate information across multiple sources, and may be only able to undertake tasks of limited complexity." A core variable in the study, the people at StatCan found, was the number of real books people had when they were in high school. Of the grads who reported having fewer than 10 books at home—which is an unimaginably and criminally low number, isn't it?—more than 30 percent were in the lower range for literacy, compared to 9 percent among those with more than 200 books. Couple that with the 2013 study by psychologists at the New School for Social Research in New York City that proved reading "writerly" literary fiction, as opposed to "readerly" pop fiction, which is predictable and unhampered by the need for the person doing the reading to actually do much thinking in the process, is good for you because—as the *Guardian* reported later that same year—it "makes you better able to connect with your fellow human beings," and you have to wonder why we're not more adamant about book learning.

A few weeks ago, I was sitting in a lecture room marking assignments while one of my classes was writing in-class analyses of a Virginia Woolf novel. What I'm about to say might violate some ethical code or hurt some feelings—which worries me only because I don't want my students thinking I'm more of a prick than I already am—but, because I think it's important, I want to share some examples of the writing I read as a kind of public-service dispatch from the front line of language and literature study at the college level.

The first notable thing I read was a paragraph written by a classic princess student in my freshman essay-writing class who must have had a medical doctor in her family because every couple of weeks she'd come to class with a note explaining why she missed the previous week. "We will consider a narrative on Meursault, who is a flaccid man who does not question about his behavior whether past or future. After demise of maternal mother, he didn't pay much attention to it as it is expected of him by the society." Whether or not she suffered from some medical condition, I don't know, but after reading sentences like this I do wonder if Nietzsche wasn't on to something big when he complained "everyone being allowed to learn to read will ruin not only writing but thinking too." I'm not supposed to think this way, I know, but I do and I really can't help it. By the time I finished identifying each mistake, her forty-four words were spattered with the volume of red befitting their linguistic savagery. Later that day I showed those two "sentences" to a colleague. We laughed. Not because we're mean to students, let alone obvious ESL students who somehow graduated from the remedial classes or passed the language entrance test—that would be wrong—but because the laughter is the only thing that stopped us from resigning ourselves, like the flaccid Meursault in that Camus novella the poor girl was trying to write about, to "the benign indifference of the world."

The second example was as existentially bizarre. It was a para-graph, from a first-year literature class, in which the first sen-tence had eight mistakes; six if you don't count the guy's spelling of both names. "The dialouging between the American and the girl in the Earnest Hemmingway's 'Hills like White Elephants' proves foreshadowingly, to readers that Jig is deciding and having her baby when she was looking at those hills even if he didn't allow her to do so at the bar." My soul goes through distressing paroxysms when I look at this word carnage, but mostly my head just really hurts because at root I'm a good person, so I try to re-assemble the mess of verbified nouns and adverb'd verbs and misplaced prepositions so I can rewrite it and maybe arrive at some "meaning" the original writer had in mind. I'm sure the kid who wrote it must have hoped, in the mystical or supersti-tious part of his brain, that I'd be able to scan his word smorgas-bord and interpret it into a meaningful sentence and, you know, just check mark it or keep reading. Like mollifying a terminally ill patient with another hit of morphine, yes, I could have done that; it *is* possible, but you've got to wonder if it's worth pro-longing the agony.

I remember reading a sentence that, like this guy's, had about eight grammar mistakes in it. The student who wrote that essay obviously failed the assignment, which meant, of course, that he was obliged to get mad at me. He asked why I failed him, and I said, "There are eight grammar mistakes in one of your sen-tences," to which he replied, "So grammar counts?" I've heard this so many times since I started teaching that I'm seriously wondering if high school English isn't a big clusterfuck of an *Oprah* episode that facilitates all manner of opinions about "feel-ings" but nothing on language itself, and when I do hear things like this, I'm tempted to paraphrase the inimitable Christopher Hitchens and say, "Everybody has a sentence inside them and in most cases that's where it should stay." But that kind of reply, if it weren't seen as a microaggression harmful to the student's sense of self-worth, would probably lead to an uncivil takedown on RateMyProfessor.com, so I went into the compulsory concil-iatory mode and told him, "Yes, grammar does count. Like wheels on a car or nails in a wooden house."

I'm not sure if I've ever had more than eight mistakes in one sentence. I might have—I don't know. I started counting only a few years ago when I noticed lots of native English speakers, like the guy who wrote the spatio-temporal vortex of a sentence on Hemingway, started sounding like ESL students because, some-where in the narrative of their young lives, their brains got un-hinged from the subject-verb-object genetic signature of complete sentences.

The third example was a sentence from an essay that was sub-mitted by a student who, after only twenty minutes of the hour I gave them to write on that day, finished his paper on *Mrs Dal-loway*. Which is itself baffling to me, given that this hour-long assignment is worth 15 percent of the final mark in a first-year post-secondary English class that students pay a few hundred bucks to take. "Clarissa who is focalised by the narrorator uses hard, complex sentences like they do on Tumblr because after all those years she is still having a hard, complex time deciding if she wants to follow her heart and marry Peter; or follow her impulse and be with Richard." Did I mention that this craft sentence, penned by a native speaker, was intended for a 15-percent essay in a first-year English Lit class that cost a bit? Sometimes—when considering sentences like this from native speakers who might very well be dyslexic but didn't provide me with the paperwork confirming the disability—I have to remind myself that I'm not a missionary whose job it is to forcibly convert primitive lettered natterings into civilized linguistic expressions. For all I know, a novel like *Mrs Dalloway*, jammed with cumulative and periodic sentences, reads to a young digital mind like their stream-of-consciousness unpunctuated sentences jammed with LOLs and emojis sometimes appear to me: like deranged tweets that don't end but take you down a rabbit hole where every thought demands to be recognized as a thought simply because it comes with words that more or less look like syntactic units because there's a period at the end of them. If you want to know what really got me, though, it was this guy's reference to Tumblr, which was an unintentional flash of brilliance bobbing in that polluted stream of words. I should have passed the kid for this, but I didn't.

A study done in 2006 by the Nielsen Norman "user experience consulting group" found that people speed-read when they're reading online, which shouldn't be surprising to anybody who's been a child, has ADD, has been sexually aroused or tried cocaine. Eye-tracking thermal scanners determined that online reading patterns, in defiance of the linear reading practices we learned in elementary school, "looks somewhat like an F." We click websites, read a sentence or two at the top of the "page," left to right, look for exciting keywords, then—likely because we're bored and tempted by another novelty—we scan down the left side of the page, looking at fewer and fewer full sentences until we decide to scroll down or click to something else. So the thermal scan notices the "F" pattern in online "reading," which is good news for online marketers, digital evangelists and hormone-fuelled adolescent brains stoked on GTA and NSFW 4chan gifs, but is probably very bad for serious deep reading and the general intellect of the human race. Last year Maryanne Wolf, a cognitive neuroscientist and author of *Proust and the Squid: The Story and Science of the Reading Brain*, said, in discussing how F-patterned online reading habits have migrated into traditional reading, "I worry that the superficial way we read during the day is affecting us when we have to read with more in-depth processing." From where I sit and work, the fact that many young people skim when they ought to be reading is old news, right up there with warnings against fast food. Our brains are evolving new circuits to skim through the mass of words and images they see online, and though that can be fun as hell, it's not always good, because reading is one activity and skimming is what you do to get the scum off the top of milk.

The pièce de résistance example that day—the fourth—was a cautionary email from a student in my novel class. After reading that sentence about the "narrorator" and "Tumblr" I had to stop and breathe. I could deal with only so much phenomenal reality before I had to open my iPhone and check my email, and when I did I read this from a student in my second-year class: "Please dont scroll all the way down a Cracked article. As they're currently running an Ad that's very triggering for phobia of symmetrycal holes in organic systems. Don't google it. Just don't. I just dont really want to see a picture of it in the large screen."

Being a prick when confronting lazy language skills that lead to frenzied interpretations and psychotic breaks has never been a problem for me, but I couldn't tell if this email was a joke the student lifted from the *Onion*, some hipster irony that flew far above my uncool radar, or what? I bushwhacked my way through the grammatically challenged request, felt so intimidated by it that I stopped myself from questioning her apparent fear and instead replied by asking her what exactly she was talking about. Apparently, it was something she saw on Cracked.com that would trigger a traumatic episode in her if I happened to show it in class. We had talked about the phenomenon of issuing "trigger warnings" in that novel class the week before—you must have heard of this practice of warning students about the stuff on a reading list that might provoke painful memories or traumas in them—and I once showed them a funny piece about writing mid-terms from the *Cracked* magazine website because I thought they'd like it. But she was seriously declaring her fear—trypophobia, I learned on *Wikipedia*, is a "pathological fear of objects with irregular patterns of holes"—so that my future lectures or discussion points wouldn't provoke some in-class PTSD episode in her and, maybe, in other students.

I've had encounters with trigger-happy students before "triggering" became an academic buzzword a few years ago. An evangelical student once cried and said he couldn't read any more of the novel I had assigned—José Saramago's beautiful *Gospel According to Jesus Christ*—because reading the first few pages made him feel he was watching his mother get raped, which I thought was a bizarrely pugnacious comparison that might have invited its own trigger warning. I had a young woman complain that *American Psycho* is a demeaning celebration of sexual violence against women but then the next week of class applaud Anne Rice's depiction of a guy being violently abused and anally fisted in one of her anonymous BDSM novels. Last year a student went to my boss after the first day of class armed with a copy of a funny little David Sedaris essay I had taught that day: he highlighted every "fuck," "shit" and "cunt" in yellow, said it was offensive and dropped the class—thankfully. Not that it matters, but I was surprised when my boss told me that he is an A+ student who is gay, like Sedaris. Last term a student complained after I spent an hour of class analyzing the striking styles in the first three sentences of Faulkner's "Dry September" because she thought it detracted from the main point of the text, which is that a middle-aged white woman was so victimized by the "toxic masculinity" of her town that she had to spread a rumour about being raped by a black man (who ends up killed by white men, which this student obviously thought was important but a relatively marginal matter in comparison to the gender issue). That same month one of my students disclosed to me and the entire class that she really appreciates trigger warnings when she sees a movie with loud noises—or, apparently, reads anything that represents loud noises—because when she was a child she was hit by a car while riding a bike. The noise, I guess, traumatized her, like a semiotic representation of mortar or artillery fire might push a soldier over some psychological edge. A young man and fellow social-justice warrior, who actually wrote his final essay on Tumblr, spoke up on her behalf, saying that the world is a cruel place and he thinks school to be a "safe place." I didn't laugh. You can't do that when you see "area of refuge" painted on floors of public buildings.

Last term I had a student who couldn't function without her screen in class. No, she didn't claim "trauma" when I asked her to shut it down but she just refused to shut it down. I'm pretty sure she never brought a pen or pencil with her, except for the mid-term and final exam. On the first day of class I did my angry Luddite schtick about their screens and I quoted some evidence, from a *Globe and Mail* story I'd read and have been pulling out for a few years, because I thought something with numbers and percentages could be convincing in a way that I can't be. *"If you don't think having your laptop screen open in front of you during class has a negative impact on your ability to listen and learn,"* I said, reading what I had—and still have—written on the syllabus—*"that's fine, but close the screen out of respect for your colleagues."* The study, by researchers at McMaster and York universities, found that "multitasking on a laptop poses a significant distraction to both users and fellow students alike." Laptop users averaged 11 percent lower on test scores, but the students who were sitting around the laptop users scored 17 percent lower. *"So!"* I said, *"No laptops in class. You are free to speak, and free to listen to what everybody else has to say, but no screens."*

But my laptop Bartleby, I remember, just sat there, mesmerized at something she was looking at on her screen, the pixel glow reflecting back at me from that sunless, technophile face that seemed to taunt me for being so obviously ignorant about this new and wonderful form of literacy, while I—and some of the other students—just looked at her, spellbound at the amazing nothingness of her listening skills. She sat there, pretty much the entire term, screen in front of her and never seeming to listen, having preferred not to shut her laptop, as if the screen were a universal human right, something as necessary as breathing and eating. She did, however, speak up whenever the conversation turned technophobic, as things did when I would do my pedagogical duty and opine about the demise of slow-reading practices and attentive reading and wonder, perhaps a bit too often, why young people think Tumblr is as valid a source of social and political knowledge as, say, a newspaper or encyclopedia.

Months later, at the end of the term, the class was engaged in a discussion of "bad parenting"—someone used the phrase in relation to something another student said about how he missed the days of quiet reading in a library that "just has books, no terminals"—when my laptop Bartleby spoke up, finally. "I'm the kind of person who can pay attention to a lot of different things at once," she announced to the class, and then she shared an anecdote about how her mother used to get mad at her when, a few years before, she would sit reading a novel at the kitchen table with her laptop open in front of her, her phone next to it, and her earbuds in her head. Her mother, apparently, just couldn't understand how she could read and understand the novel when she was also paying attention to her laptop and music.

And neither could I. But laptop Bartleby would have none of it, which was the most startling aspect of this exchange. When confronted with an argument that refutes the intellectual function of the entertainment consoles they've been weaned on but haven't been able to let go of for the purpose of attentive learning, or when confronted with something that sounds like authoritative or common sense, she—like every other screen lover I've ever had to deal with in class—ignores it, deciding simply on the basis of her own will that she must be right.

There are lots of reasons for these little melodramatic flare-ups of panic. Maybe the average nineteen- or twenty-two-year-old is, in fact, a lot more like a twelve-year-old than an adult, or maybe it's a confluence of great big political and economic forces. The absence of jobs, property values that keep kids locked in their parents basements where the computers are, and so on. Most of all, I think, it's that the knee-jerk fast reading and writing people do online—on Twitter and Tumblr—is migrating offline, virus-like, to the classroom and pretty much everywhere else. That's the real allergy of reading.

Hot for Teacher: What Fifty Shades of Grey Taught Me about Scandalous Grammar, Salacious Women and the Conflation of Culture and Economics

> I pull him deeper into my mouth so I can feel him at the back of my throat and then to the front again. My tongue swirls around the end. He's my very own Christian Grey-flavored popsicle. I suck harder and harder.... My inner goddess is doing the merengue with some salsa moves.
>
> —E.L. James, *Fifty Shades of Grey*

Last year I spent a few months posing, more or less anonymously, as a guy called "English Prof" on a website, frequented almost exclusively by women, devoted to that remarkably inane blockbuster *Fifty Shades of Grey*. I created my online persona in April 2012, just when the novel's success was attracting the kind of frenzied media hype reserved for celebrity sex scandals and other juvenile frivolities. Now, teaching bad literature isn't in my job description, but I ventured into this tawdry world of "mommy porn" and "clit-lit" fandom because I was teaching a sophomore course that I called "Sex Sells, Literature Doesn't: Advertising, Branding & the Fictions of the Market" and so I wanted to collect first-hand accounts about the book from its hardcore readers. Over the course of a few months, though, what started as a casual experiment with this novel in the name of higher education challenged and even changed my prudish understanding of language, sex and marketing.

Conceived in the juvenile world of *Twilight* fan fiction, where young, anonymous pop-culture junkies write derivative tales about Stephanie Meyer's vampire stories, and eventually published as a discreet e-book, where it got the attention of many more older women who wanted to read it but didn't want to be seen reading it in public, E.L. James's novel walked out of the closet of cultural inconsequentiality when it was published by Vintage in April of 2011. No novel—not *The Da Vinci Code* and not even *Harry Potter*—has ever drawn as much crowd-sourced attention and media coverage as *Fifty Shades* did in the winter and spring of 2012. The *Wall Street Journal* reported that between March and July of that year, *Fifty Shades* accounted for one in five of *all* fiction sales in the U.S., which is remarkable. I was thrilled to see that a novel could monopolize public discussion at a time when literature never seemed less important, but like most reasonable people who read, I was irritated that it had to be *this* novel. In January 2012 Andrew Gallix wrote in an essay for the *Guardian* (subtitled "The Death of Literature") that "we are no longer writing literature's conclusion but its 'epilogue,'" and if that's true, I thought, what gives with this derivative bit of masturbatory pulp? How can a culture that gives so much attention to such a silly sex story not be headed for oblivion?

James appeared on *The Today Show* in April of that year and, in a gentle, somewhat disturbing matronly tone that caught me slightly off guard, addressed all that spanking, binding and dom-sub fetish sex in her book that had everybody talking by saying that once a woman's job and the house and kids were all looked after, "it's nice for someone else to be in charge for a bit." And that was the breathtakingly simple explanation of why her hero, Christian Grey, the fabulously well-to-do sex-god billionaire with a fondness for administering punishment to women in his "Red Room of Pain"—but, savvy alpha male that he is, not before signing a "non-disclosure agreement"—manages to seduce the virginal heroine, English-literature student Anastasia Steele, and millions of other very real women readers.

I will admit that it was very hard to teach a book like this without poking fun at the formulaic plot that mashes clichéd Harlequin Romance with even more clichéd RedTube porn, the banal characterizations, the overuse of simple sentences, and the periodic attempts to punctuate all those moisture-induced scenes with literary gravitas by tossing in metaphors and allusions to classic novels and music that anybody with some rudimentary knowledge of culture should know. It was even harder to explain to a college class—five men and twenty-five women—why this novel we were "studying" was at that very moment in history being read, thought and talked about by so many women outside the classroom, mostly because so much of the discussion centred on that bamboozling question of whether a book about a relationship in which the fictional female has a fascination for sexually submitting to the male dominant is good or bad for real women, and whether it matters in some sociological manner that women readers are the ones who pushed this book to the top of the *New York Times* bestseller list even before it appeared in stores.

I guess that's the main reason I created my persona on the *Fifty Shades* fan page. When I first found all the online chatter I felt a mixture of disgust at my own voyeurism and naïve incredulity at the discrepancy between what I expected to get from the women and what most of them wanted to talk about with me. I felt like a fully clothed anthropologist, notebook in hand, walking among a tribe of naked women trying to get their attention with long-winded questions about grammar and style when all they really wanted to talk about was tall, rakish gentlemen who were rich and hung like field-grazing farm animals. I formally introduced myself in a post, told them that I was teaching the book to college students in Canada, and then asked if any would mind answering the questions my students and I devised. I assured them I wasn't some pervert infiltrating their chat for some depraved reason and offered to share my real name and phone number with any who asked. I also told them I'd use their responses in my lectures when we got to talking about the novel in class. There were dozens of enthusiastic first responses to the list of questions we came up with, though ultimately there weren't as many answers as I hoped to get, and this is probably because the questions weren't really the fun kind that allowed for the overheated wish-fulfillment sex-fantasy discourse that seemed typical of their site.

If "literature" is writing that has "redeeming literary merit"—that is, if it makes good use of language in the execution of a story and character development—does this novel count as literature? That, basically, was the first question we asked, and some of the responses left me and probably some of the students wondering why we even bothered to ask. *"My opinion on the literary merit of fifty shades is lacking in my opinion but although the writing was bad in some aspects i was still able to read it and enjoyed it in spite of the mistakes,"* one woman wrote in one of the more polished responses. Another one with an aversion for uppercased letters and some of the habitual linguistic misdemeanours of the age said this: "*i read bks like this and there the same, the scenes aren't supposed to grab you with words who has time for that when your all hot from the sex, lol.*" Do we really still need to prove that all the amateur talk that swirls around the sexed-up parts of the Web 2.0 is impairing our ability to think and write?

I have this grammar schtick I do when I teach novels with lots of sex scenes. I use it as a way to illustrate what the concept of "merit" means in both a legal and literary context, but also to show that *any* book, even very badly written hand-to-crotch masturbatory pulp like *Fifty Shades*, can be read from a formal point of view. I put what's supposed to be an explicit passage on the screen and deconstruct it by pointing out, say, the complex-compound sentences and the hypotactic style. Nothing could be more unsexy, but it's been a useful little exercise because with a good writer like D.H. Lawrence or Angela Carter, the tempo and rhythm of the sex—seduction to orgasm to post-coital whatever—aren't just delivered in list-like descriptions that point to some reality we're supposed to believe exists out there because we've suspended our disbelief; the sex is in the periodic and cumulative sentence structures, in the suspended syntax and narrative morphology of paragraphs. What's hot, in other words, is always a function of the language, which needs to be *read* prior to any phenomenological arousal that takes place, whereas in pornish pop fluff like James's novel, it's in the highly patterned hallucinated reality that's *consumed* before any reading takes place.

Here are a couple of exceptionally bad sentences from *Fifty Shades* in which Christian tells Ana to say hello to his not-so-little friend: "I want you to become well acquainted, on first name terms if you will, with my favorite and most cherished part of my body. I'm very attached to this." Here's another, this one from Ana's interior monologue: "Sitting beside me, he gently pulls my sweatpants down again. *Up and down like whores' drawers*, my subconscious remarks bitterly. In my head, I tell her where to go. Christian squirts baby oil into his hand and then rubs my behind with careful tenderness—from makeup remover to soothing balm for a spanked ass, who would have thought it was such a versatile liquid?" And one more from Ana, who is here having her ass manipulated: "His finger circled my puckered love cave. 'Are you ready?' he mewled, smirking at me like a mother hamster about to eat her three-legged young."

Anybody who's ever done sex, whether well or poorly, knows that sex is rhetorically structured on a narrative that goes from complexity to simplicity, from the sophistication of rhetorical seduction, where we use sentences with subjects, verbs and objects, to the prelinguistic sucking and licking and squelching noises, where we don't need much more than verb-verb-verb articulations. The curmudgeonly literary critic George Steiner once said the problem with sex writing is that it's too public. Pornographers subvert our "last, vital privacy" and "do our imagining for us. They take away the words that were of the night and shout them over the roof-tops, making them hollow." I think Steiner's right, but part of me—the part that went "what the fuck?" when I read that line about Ana's love cave and the mewling hamster—wonders if this just means that some people for whatever reason feel compelled to publicize their allegiance to sexuality in terms of primal stupidities. But then, like porn and pop fiction, *Fifty Shades* isn't really meant to be read but to be *consumed*, or lasciviously flipped through until you get to the next hot part, perhaps those marked by sticky and discoloured dog-eared pages.

More interesting even than what the women fans had to say about the "literary" quality of the novel was what they said about the dominant-submissive relationship and its potential effect on gender. The loudest criticism of the novel, which was also its strongest marketing point, was that it set the women's movement back decades. I admit that my own smug—and, I'm sure, sexist—response to it was that it's just kind of dumb for women to fantasize about sexual submission and that years of Gloria Steinem essays and gender sensitivity should have moved us away from ideologically regressive representations like we get with Christian and Anastasia. Well, theoretically speaking anyways, because the master-servant dialectic still endures across so much of the culture industry, just as it seems to in actual human sex lives, or at least how we articulate it in culture. In April 2012 Katie Roiphe wrote a splendid article in *Newsweek* called "Spanking Goes Mainstream." In it she wondered about the current popularity of the sexual submission theme in *Fifty Shades*—and in works like the popular HBO TV show *Girls* and David Cronenberg's recent film *A Dangerous Method*—arguing that "the erotic imagination does not submit to politics." Lots of people jumped all over her because they thought Roiphe was giving the thumbs up to female submission, and *Newsweek* capitalized on the controversy to come by splashing a picture of a sexy, blindfolded woman across its front cover. Next to her were the lines "The Fantasy Life of Working Women. Why Surrender is a Feminist Dream." It's interesting, Roiphe noted, that so many women are "eagerly consuming myriad and disparate fantasies of submission" at a time in history when, in bigger economic and educational terms, they "are less dependent or subjugated than before." Yes, that says something about modern women "that nearly everyone wishes wasn't said"—and she's so right—but Roiphe concluded—also rightly, I think—"maybe sex and aggression should not, and probably more to the point, cannot be untangled."

This business of sexual submission and women and gender politics is a real melon scratcher of a conundrum, and it's an issue any guy would be squeamish talking about in front of a class of mostly women undergraduate students. When I read the Roiphe essay a month before I was scheduled to teach the novel, I wondered how I was supposed to talk about the apparent popularity of female submission in the classroom. Would it be considered a microaggression by some hypervigilant student who's taken a women's studies course? When I was a graduate student I took courses at Osgoode Hall Law School and took to heart Catharine MacKinnon's argument that heterosexual sex was an awful lot like rape because male sexuality is "activated by violence against women and expresses itself in violence against women." I had to do quite the mental backbend when, twenty years later, liberated young women seemed to be embracing submission. But honestly, and philosophically, ever since I read de Sade's *Philosophy in the Bedroom*, I've thought that real power, not some romantic concept of liberal democracy, structures what happens in our sex lives, and as much as I think that that's probably what it's like in most bedrooms, it's not like I can go around saying this sort of thing to young people, even if all those women who bought the 65 million copies of *Fifty Shades* since early 2013 seemed to be saying it.

So in the interests of putting front-line reality bytes into a very different academic context, we asked about the purported *effects* a book can have on readers. The gist of the question was this: "As a reader, do you think you *are* what you read?" I pulled the line from an op-ed piece I read in the *New York Times* years earlier; I've always wondered why most people think the words that populate the context of their lives—what they read—don't have any effect on how and what they think. The responses from the fan site fit the stereotype. *"No, I'm not what I read! But I think this book can actually help women discover their inner goddess again that may have been sleeping,"* one wrote in her response to me. *"I think it ignites a spark between married couples again as it did for me and my hubby. We talked about the book and engaged in some of the things that the book engaged in making for a more exciting, intimate relationship. I think of this book as more of a self-help romance sex novel."* It's a contradiction to deny that a novel has consequences on your real life and celebrate it by saying that it spices up your real sex life, but obviously I wasn't about to go around wagging my finger at this reader's improved bedroom activities. Another said, *"I don't feel that I am what I read. Why do I read erotica, mysteries, true crime, biographies? Because the plot interests me. I love the novel* Mommy Dearest. *That doesn't mean I'm looking to physically, verbally and mentally abuse my children. I enjoyed* Fifty Shades. *Do I have a desire to be tied up and spanked? No. For me, reading is pure escapism. You can escape into worlds you know nothing about, possibly worlds you want nothing to do with. It's a break from the day-to-day B.S. of life."*

Most of the fans responded with the familiar refrain that literature is escapism and that novels—even novels that repeat clichéd sex practices and are only intended to *arouse*, which is of course a pretty real and powerful physiological effect—can't make us think or do anything. Sadly, most people probably think the same. Thomas Frank has an essay in the March 2013 issue of *Harper's* in which he put forward the logical but unpopular argument that works of art—whether movies, first-person shooter games, plays or novels like *Fifty Shades*—aren't without real consequences. "To insist on a full, pristine separation of the dramatic imagination from the way humans actually behave is to fly in the face of nearly everything we know about cultural history," he says. Only the most narcissistic libertarians and other ego-driven maniacs think their actions and behaviour are unsusceptible to the influence of art and fiction. But reading Shakespeare plays or *Twilight* obviously changes how we think of romance and love, Ayn Rand novels lead us to think that the pursuit of wealth is a good and fine thing and that governments are always bad, and Harlequin Romances and online porn will structure how we think and act in amorous situations. Still, people generally dislike thinking that their lives—especially their swelling and thrusty flesh lives—are manufactured in any way by the culture industry.

The *Fifty Shades* fan page demonstrated to me how something as apparently innocuous as a bodice-tearing novel can have real effects, even if those effects are measured in terms of this "fantasy" life we live in real time in bedrooms with others or in bathrooms or elsewhere when alone. I logged in every day for the three months I kept my profile and on most of those days it seemed to me like a great number of fans spent hours and hours enthusiastically talking about the book and about their own sex lives, wondering how the fictional sex and romance in the novel matched or didn't match their experiences and fantasizing about all kinds of scenarios in which their lives might resemble the more exciting structures of fiction. I mean, seriously, when has a work of fiction ever had *more* of an effect? The famous German playwright Bertolt Brecht once said that the problem with the bourgeoisie is that it's entirely passive when confronted with art. Instead of sitting in your seat passively watching a play, politely clapping and then leaving the theatre as the same person you were when you arrived earlier, he said you ought to actively engage with the theatre like you engage with a sporting event. You should watch a play, for example, like you'd watch a boxing match or hockey game. Interact, get physical, yell and talk back, feel it happening. The effect should be visceral and it should be political, too, and—whether you love it or loathe it—by this measure the *Fifty Shades* fan page was nothing if not deeply engaged, though I'm sure Brecht would be critical of the life it simulates.

One day I logged onto the fan page and found this animated post by a reader who, like Anastasia, thought lots about oral sex and had a fetish for unrestrained punctuation. *"Good morning!!!!! What are we gonna discuss today???? I can think of a topic!!!! I don't mind giving BJ, but hate the taste and texture!!!! How can I either make it more palatable or fake a swallow???? Why do guys want you to swallow anyway???? I looked up the nutritional value and it's loaded with protein!!!!! What do you think????"* I may have made a mistake with the number of exclamation and question marks, but you get the point. The responses vindicated a couple of the claims about the popularity of the novel—that it allows women to speak openly about their sex lives and that it was heating up a lot of otherwise cooled bedrooms, both of which are good—I guess. *"Sucking cock makes me hot"* and *"My husband's penis has been in my mouth more in the last two weeks than it was in our first 7 years of marriage"* were the first comments in the thread that day. The rest—there were about seventy of them—sounded just as roused and just as ridiculous, but there they were, online, in all their visceral thought, though with very little political glory.

Over the course of my stay on the fan page some of the women sent me their own *Fifty Shades*-inspired "erotica" and asked for feedback. I imagine they did this because I told them that I once interviewed a writer of erotica about her steamy novel that also made gobs of money. I responded as best as I could but confined my comments to the technical points I write in the margins of student papers, though I knew that genuine critical commentary had no place in the easily offended world of online fandom and blogs. Surprisingly—or maybe not—a few of the writers started getting flirty, but that kind of communication is built into the context of all anonymous social network chatter, isn't it? One fan-cum-writer wrote a "story" called "Hot for Teacher" and asked me to "edit" it for her, though it was clear that she was more interested in provoking my sexual imagination than getting feedback on grammar and narrative structure. For as long as it takes to read a few emails and scan through a vapid story about a first-person narrator who, for reasons probably indebted way more to cultural influences than the author's own inner goddess would ever admit, wants to be tied up and spanked by her "professor" because she's been a "bad girl" and not submitted her essay to his specifications, I was a little provoked, maybe even a tad aroused. It was all very interesting, and I was about as narcissistically ego stroked as an adult can get when someone likes their Facebook photo or posts something like "hawt" beneath it.

For some reason, that particular scribe sent me a picture of herself that was, judging by the outfit she was wearing in it, supposed to help me visualize that already very literal-minded roman-a-clef she'd penned about the teacher and his errant essay writer, but this wasn't as surprising as it should have been to me, because pretty much everything that circulated around the *Fifty Shades* fan page was shot through with a compulsory hypersexual energy. One of the other women writers eventually—and by "eventually" I mean within a few weeks of her appearance on the fan page—had her story published as an e-book, and this did surprise me because the story was cobbled together from posts she'd made on the fan page in the months I was there. I looked it up on Amazon.com, and there it was. The first reader's comment was *"I didn't put it down until I was done, now I can't wait til my husband cums home!"* What started out as salaciousness was getting, by degrees, more and more tawdry. What made me delete my profile from the *Fifty Shades* fan page wasn't that the school term was drawing to an end; rather, it was a set of photos of two diapered infants, one boy and one girl, playing with a length of rope. They were, as I understand it, the offspring of one of the more vocal members. The caption she put beneath the photo was "They start early" or something to that effect. Maybe this sort of tabloid tastelessness is inevitable in sex-obsessed online communities. It certainly felt to me as though the internal law of the fan page—though it was buzzing with all that sex talk, which was supposed to be good and empowering and all that wonderfully liberating stuff—was that it needed to get more provocative and scandalous with each post, and in that sense it was to be expected.

It's been said that the benefit of online communication is that it's democratic and liberates our previously repressed selves. That's a very pretty thought and there must be some truth to it, but like most pretty thoughts, it's an ideological mystification. What's not true is that, prior to the web and its abundant anonymous online communities, we were a bunch of puritans just waiting for the chance to think and write salaciously. Chuck Klosterman, in his excellent book *Sex, Drugs, and Cocoa Puffs,* pointed out that the Internet, saturated as it is with naked people with their naked thoughts, accomplished not the liberation of human sexuality but the normalization of amateur sexuality. "Were there really millions of women in 1986 turning to their husbands and saying, 'You know, I would love to have total strangers masturbate to images of me deep-throating a titanium dildo, but there's simply no medium for that kind of entertainment. I guess we'll just have to sit here and watch Falcon Crest?" His point is that all that groin-enlivening stuff online, in words and pictures, wasn't allowed by technology; it was *produced* by it. The media is the message.

Fifty Shades is a poor novel with a dim-witted view of sexuality and an at-best milquetoast or vanilla concept of BDSM and, contrary to what most of its fans told me, it did have quite an effect on a lot of lives, both real and imaginary, if by "effect" we mean how a novel can make you think and act when nobody's around to watch you. But that effect needs to be measured in economic, not just literary, terms because the novel, though it can never be called "Literature," had this massive trickle-down effect, and not only on its readers who took it as a sex-drive solution. One of the first women to respond to my initial request when I set out on the experiment turned out to be my most eloquent interlocutor for the time I kept my profile. Her response to the question "Are you surprised that this book is being taught in a second-year college English class?" reminded me of the motivation that lay beneath much of that make-believe sex chatter of that fan page. "I think it's fantastic you are teaching this at the college level. I own a sex toy party plan company and am ecstatic about this book going mainstream to the general public. It was only after a friend of mine who doesn't like to read told me how much people were talking about the book at her parties that I decided to pick it up and read it from a business standpoint for my company. I am now going crazy with the marketing of products. Yay!"

Fifty Shades of Grey has the appearance of literature only because it sort of has a plot and is bound by front and back covers, but it nonetheless marks a remarkable moment in the history of fiction, not because it lays bare all that romance and sex and canned talking that happens between Anastasia and Christian, but because it opens up a mesmerizing trend in crowd-sourced cultural economics. The *New York Post* reported a spike in sales of duct tape and rope among women when the novel was getting all that press in May of 2012; a Seattle hotel offered a Fifty Shades of Romance weekend package that included a deluxe room and a map of the novel's local literary landmarks; an English hotel chain issued a press release suggesting it would replace Gideon's bibles in all its bedside table drawers with *Fifty Shades*; the *Globe and Mail* featured a quarter-page ad from Random House with the slogan "Get Tied up in Fifty Shades of Grey"; the novel, unsurprisingly, opened the way to other sexed-up popular versions of classics like *Jane Eyre Laid Bare* and *Fifty Shades of Louisa May*. And a year later, a Canadian *Fifty Shades* knock-off called *SECRET* is at the top of bestseller lists at home. Inexplicably—or probably not—I happened to be travelling when I was finishing this piece, and one warm, grey day, while walking around a gas-station café on an autoroute south of Lisbon, I stopped to look at a little bookshelf in the corner of the shop. Copies of *Cinquenta Tons de Cinza* occupied the entire top row. "Yay!" indeed.

Julia's Nipples and God's Barometer

In 1800 an English newspaper called the *Evangelical Magazine* pub-lished a visual aid intended to help people figure out their moral worth. They called it "God's barometer," and it assigned different numerical values—ranging from positive 100 to negative 100—to various virtuous and sinful behaviours, with "Glory" occupying the topmost position and "Perdition" the bottom. The higher your actions ranked on the chart, the more moral you were and the better off your immortal soul. So, if I were the type of person who enjoyed "luxurious entertainment" or "carnal company," the barom-eter would rank me 90 points beneath Glory; if "fashion" and "levity in conversation" were my vices, I'd be slightly better off at 80 below. But what drew me to this early version of a pictogram is where it ranked literature. If my sin was a "love of novels," then I'd come in at 110 degrees below Glory, which was just a spit away from adultery and lewd conduct and, remarkably, only a stone's throw away from eternal damnation in hell.

Such sanctimonious gossip about the depravity of literature is as old as the hills, but not all of the gossips in the late years of the Enlightenment were English evangelical crackers. Even the French, who always seem to enjoy the finer things like sex and lit-erature so much more than the rest of us, occasionally worked themselves into lathers over the fleshy sins of fiction. In the mid-dle of the eighteenth century, the renowned liberal man of reason Denis Diderot said that the new genre of the novel "presents a threat to the tastes and morals of readers." And then there was the peculiar French doctor, M.D.T. Bienville who, a few years later in his 1771 book *Nymphomania, or a Dissertation Concerning the Furor Uterinus*, tried to find an empirical connection between novels and sexual perversion. The "furor uterinus," he said, exists in all women—young, married, widows, whores and especially servants—but is only triggered when they do things that overstimulate their delicate nerve fibres, like eating rich foods and chocolate, masturbating or "reading luxurious novels."

Today, guys like Diderot and Bienville—both philosophically inclined to materialism, the belief that how we think and act is determined by our actual conditions rather than ideas—come across like joyless prudes who just wanted to make people stop having fun. Even the most uptight eighteenth-century virgin probably would have thought a life without chocolate, masturbation and novels exceptionally uninteresting. But what made the evangelist meteorologists, the philosopher and the doctor target novels as provocative fetish items during the age of liberalism and Casanova? It couldn't have been that these guys hated sex—most of them were married with children and were therefore at least nominally interested in copulation—so maybe it was something about the genre of the novel itself—"a perpetual quest for reality," as Lionel Trilling once defined it—that pushed their hot buttons and made them think the sins of the flesh and the sins of the page were one and the same thing.

Before novels came onto the pop cultural scene in England 300 years ago, there was a lot more literature about desire and raw body-on-body experiences than our post-Victorian minds think. In the middle of the seventeenth century an English priest named Robert Herrick wrote a poem called "Upon the Nipples of Julia's Breast," which is hardly raunchy by our standards but is still more suited to Hooters than to the High Church:

Have ye beheld (with much delight)
A red rose peeping through a white?
Or else a cherry double grac'd
Within a lily center-plac'd?
Or ever mark'd the pretty beam?
A strawberry shows half-drown'd in cream?

We could pull a literary fast one and call this a sustained metaphorical reflection on the nurturing faculty of the female form but that would just repeat the schoolroom hallucination that literature, especially poetry, has to be about immortal truths and not mortal flesh and its capacity to arouse. Yes, there is art in the organic symbolism and rhyming couplets, but the poem was written by a tit man, a seventeenth-century Russ Meyer who was driving at that vital part of heterosexual male fantasy life that involves living to catch a glimpse of a woman's breasts. In "Upon Julia's Breasts" he treated this fantasy material in a more explicit manner, although the sex is encased in lofty language:

DISPLAY thy breasts, my Julia, there let me
Behold that circummortal purity;
Between whose glories, there my lips I'll lay
Ravish'd, in that fair Via Lactea

Here is an Anglican cleric who believed that lust is to be expected in people, an attitude that is still foreign to some of us today but one that was characteristic of a pre-enlightened time in history when frankness about sexuality was the norm rather than the exception.

An then there was the popular rake, the Earl of Rochester, whose repertoire of scandalous four-letter words was so vast that it makes the most profane bitchin' song sound like a Pat Boone number. In one of his poems we get a savvy woman of high rank asking her adviser how she might graciously satisfy a craving for cock:

> Quoth the Duchess of Cleveland to counselor Knight,
> "I'd fain have a prick, knew I how to come by't
> I desire you'll be secret and give your advice:
> Though cunt be not coy, reputation is nice."

There was three centuries ago, and there still exists today in the imagined lives of the bourgeoisie, a strange belief that women never, *ever*, talked "dirty" like this, or wrote about sex so bluntly, especially not 200 years before Queen Victoria unintentionally lent her name to prudery. But there was the remarkable Aphra Behn, the first woman ever to make a living as a writer. She was quite good at writing stylized erotica that shocked readers with its buxom frankness. One of her poems, "The Disappointment," reads like a script for a lewd Viagra commercial, even if it is gussied up in pastoral language. After a few stanzas of feeling up, Cloris—which sounds an awful lot like?—finally makes a move on her boy-toy Lysander:

> Her timorous Hand she gently laid
> Or guided by Design or Chance,
> Upon that fabulous Pirapus,

That Potent God...
Finding that God of her desires
Disarmed of all his awful fires.

A hundred years later, after the Protestants consolidated their power in England, it might have been immoral for a woman writer to write this way, let alone for one of her female characters to move a hand anywhere near a guy's hard-on. Even today a poem about a woman who dares to go down probably wouldn't go down well, not as literature anyways, although in television culture, women like Samantha, Miranda, Charlotte and Carrie talk about and do this sort of thing all the time in the name of a new sort of feminism that really isn't as new as they think. Behn's Cloris—"Her loose thin robes, through which appear / A shape designed for love and play"—certainly wanted to do it, even though, against the odds, she finds a limp biscuit instead of a freestanding maypole.

The point is that Behn is putting out an idea that may have been troubling for some readers in her time but was nonetheless accepted in her work, which is that women can like sex and should be unafraid of doing what turns them on. Think of the French art critic Catherine Millet's recent bestseller, *The Sexual Life of Catherine M.*, and take away that anomie-styled laconic overkill—"really like sucking men's cocks"—and you get the picture. Behn's poem doesn't offer up straight oral sex or a fuck scene; it's like a beckoning finger pointing to a keyhole through which we see a woman "abandoned by her pride and shame" trying to get into a guy's pants.

But it wasn't because they were poets that writers like Behn and Rochester were licensed to put sex to paper. That license mostly came from the sex-positive social context in which they wrote, a time when lewdness and debauchery may have been moral terms but didn't really stick as terms of literary judgment. The Stuart monarchy had just regained power from the Puritans, only a decade after the Puritans had chopped off a Stuart king's head and did some seriously puritanical cleaning of English society—closing the theatres, making adultery punishable by death, outlawing flashing clothing, and smashing the stained glass in Catholic churches because it impeded our literal connectedness to God, and so on. The Restoration period the Puritans so despised, by contrast, was a decadent era of cool rich people behaving badly and a culture that condoned a run on ribald publications. The literati snubbed that low-church Protestant smugness by writing about sex as if it actually happened in the world and wasn't just a repulsive detail that had to be hidden away—unless of course it was half-veiled in a witty double-entendre. In a way, people like Herrick, Rochester and Behn were like sophisticated pro-porn urbanites today, those wealthy and well-educated people who make their boring lives more interesting by keeping arty sex books like *The Beauty of Fetish* on their coffee tables or hanging a collection of Barbara Nitke's "refined" S&M photos on their wall, or by renting porn videos with meaningful plots on weekends.

The trouble was that the Puritan turn in culture never fully went away, even if the Puritans did. After the Glorious Revolution of 1689, when the last Stuart king and his dapper Catholic acolytes were exiled once and for all by a band of Dutch Protestants and businessmen, there was a revolution in literary culture. It pitted the Puritan belief of beauty-resistant simplicity against the glamour of *haute couture*, a journalistic passion for facts against legend and sacred narratives, and common-sense literal thinking against fancy books with all those metaphors. As an antidote to salacious Restoration drama—*Marriage à la Mode* and *Love in a Tub*—we got sentimental comedies, where decent middle-class people with no connection to nobility grappled with worldly problems and resolved them in typically Christian terms, with an eye to upholding the new ideals of the Protestant middle class, like chastity, the bliss of domestic life, the value of hard work and the sanctity of property.

The ultimate remedy for top-heavy poetry and decadent drama was the novel, the literary form characteristic of the bourgeois age, with its emphasis on individuals making their way in a material world of work and property, its vindication of a secular culture of commerce and trade, and its affirmation of the privacy necessary for reading. Built on an aesthetic of formal realism—literal language purged of metaphorical excess, everyday characters, a matter-of-fact plot developing in real time and in real places—these novels aimed at a correspondence to the world "out there." That's why novelists drew on Puritan arguments like those of literalist preacher Richard Baxter, who believed that "painted" language—everything from similes and irony to classical allusions and legendary plots—is "like the Painted Glass in windows that keep out the light." You can see here that literal and metaphorical language relate to each other like the relatively new Protestantism to older and more ornate Roman Catholicism.

Writers like Daniel Defoe, the journalist whose stories were among the first novels, certainly took this stuff seriously, and that's why his work is full of descriptions of smelly old London and real-life sketches of joe-average types. *Robinson Crusoe,* which most of us have heard of but few have read, is a novel because its narrator empirically classifies and lists everything on his island, as if producing for the very first time a quantifiable world with its precise rhythms of time and space. Like the reliable FedEx employee Chuck in the Robert Zemeckis film *Cast Away*—played by Hollywood's multipurpose everyman hero Tom Hanks—the original Crusoe was a man of facts, not fantasy. Not once does he turn his attention to the simple fact of his own body and its passions and needs, but that's because Defoe, hardcore Protestant and vehement anti-Catholic that he was, saw sex as an irrational element of life—like the stained glass in a window—that stood in the way of a good work ethic. Always the sexless capitalist, when after twenty-four years Crusoe finally notices that he's all alone on that Caribbean island, all that he ends up praying for is a male slave to help him put things in order. The man Friday is the cannibal Carib Indian that Fate sends him.

At times Defoe's novels did offend moralists, and not only because these people tend always to disapprove of new forms of cultural expression. Novels were different than earlier genres because they were consciously about an empirical world in which everything that goes on in our heads comes from our *senses*, and the more indebted to sense a genre is, the closer it gets to *sensuality*. "Real" means everything there is, after all, including the dirty things and repressed needs. Add to this the fact that in poetry and romance and drama you get crafted lines and periodic sentences, ideas shaped to a controlling voice, whereas in novels the lines are looser and the sentences can accumulate like a chain of events rising into a climactic plot, and leave you feeling as though the naked physical world has just come onto the page in front of you and collapsed there.

One novel that was criticized for just this sort of thing is *Love in Excess*, which along with *Robinson Crusoe* was one of the two most popular novels in the first half of the eighteenth century. Written in 1719 by Eliza Haywood, it's an early Harlequin Romance shot through with fragments of female erotica. Here, for example, we have Melliora, a girl who wouldn't think of making merry with the sexy beast Count D'Elmont in her waking life, having a wet dream about him while he stands there playing the voyeur, getting his codpiece all engorged as he listens to her talk through her moans:

Imagination at this time was active, and brought the charming Count much nearer than indeed he was, and he, stooping to the bed, and gently laying his face close to hers, that action concurring at that instant, with her dream, made her throw her arm about his neck, and in a soft and languishing voice, cry out "Oh D'elmont, cease, cease to charm, to such a height—Life cannot bear these raptures."—And then again, embracing him yet closer, "O! too, too lovely Count—extatick ruiner!"

Thirty years later Haywood's novel *Betsy Thoughtless* was called "immoral" for a bedroom scene that pales in comparison to her earlier panting narrative of nocturnal emission. The titillation in the passage above is in the sexual expressiveness of the dream: the orgasmic crescendo in her voice and the rhythmic patter of punctuation requires no footnote to tell us what she was probably doing with her other hand. Put this together with the next scene, where the Count takes off his waistcoat and pushes himself down on Melliora's heaving, bare breasts, and we have a literary dry-hump session. And then the *really* naughty bit, which is the female narrator's compulsive affirmation of the matter-over-mind power of male lust: "I believe there are very few men that in such tempting circumstance would not have lost all thought, but those, which the present opportunity inspired."

Sure, there were novels that pushed sex from dreams and suggestive narrative digressions into the full light of day. Like *Fanny Hill*, a raunchy story from the 1740s that John Cleland sold for twenty guineas to a London bookseller, who then turned around and made £10,000 from it. Loved by readers but loathed by moralizers, *Fanny* surfaced in 1963 after 200 years underground only to have an American court declare it obscene and forbid its sale. Granted, it's an erotic potboiler featuring thirty-nine sex scenes with ingenious modifications to the fellatio-cunnilingus-copulation structure of basic porn—including one where Fanny does it upside down—but there are few of the *oohh, yeah, fuck me harder* laugh-out-loud sentences characteristic of modern masturbatory pulp or lurid websites. And you don't get the feeling, as you do in a lot of written porn, that the writer sees language as an obstacle to describing the discharge of bodily fluids into one hole or another. Instead, the writing is the pith and substance of the sex. This is Fanny telling us why her story needs to be explicit. It's an explanation that could easily work as a statement of realistic intent for most eighteenth-century novels:

Truth! Stark, naked truth is the word; and I will not so much as take the pains to bestow the strip of a gauze wrapper on it, but paint situations such as they actually rose to me in nature, and you have too much sense, too much knowledge of the ORIGINALS themselves, to sniff prudishly and out of character at the PICTURES of them.

In other words, this is a novel so it must be truthful because that's what novels are, and the truth of the matter is that sometimes people get naked and fuck and suck and do pleasing things to other people's bodies, and nobody who has done this in real life should have a hissy fit about a book that narrates these actions with style and panache in language.

Part of the allure of the novel is that the arousal happens *in the language*—Cleland wrote *Fanny Hill* without using any four-letter profanities—and the way it renders the rustle of a dress coming off or the quick intake of a breath that comes when a hand or finger moves into position. Here is Fanny thinking back to when her friend Phoebe introduced her to the joys of mutual masturbation when she first arrived in London:

Then the cavity to which she guided my hand easily received it; and as soon as she felt it within her, she moved herself to and fro, with so rapid a friction that I presently withdrew it, wet and clammy, when instantly Phoebe grew more composed, after two or three sighs, and heart-fetched Oh's! and giving me a kiss that seemed to exhale her soul through her lips, she replaced the bedclothes over us.

Maybe Cleland gets female sexuality all wrong—who knows. Blundering though it may be, his description of an orgasm as an exhalation of the soul is still one of the metaphorically finer moments of sexual ornamentation I've ever read. But it was borderline vulgar at that time, too. Although one person using a helping hand to get another person off was more "normal" then than it is now, all forms of masturbation were at the time starting to be diagnosed as "the heinous sin of self-pollution," as one medical book put it. In any case, it wasn't the lesbian sex scenes that ran Cleland into trouble. When he and his novel were dragged before the Privy Council, the material that seemed to cause the most offence was the one description of two men going at it, which is just as revealing as the relative permissiveness of other sexualities.

Part of the popularity of Cleland's novel is that it was one of many salacious satires of Samuel Richardson's thunky novel *Pamela*, a book prized by teachers for its realistic letter-writing style, or "writing to the moment," even though none of the moments in this story about a rakish squire trying to bed his virtuous maid had anything to do with sex. Not directly, anyways. *Pamela*—who is like an eighteenth-century Britney Spears, only a lot smarter—obsessively talks about her virginity as if it, and nothing else, will guarantee her a place in the sweet hereafter, but what the satirists picked up on was that the scene structure, cadence and dialogue verge on a kind of tabloid titillation because the poor girl is always *just barely* escaping rape and sexual assault. It was a case of literary blue balls, in other words. If titillation was at least part of the point—and it had to be, since the book was basically a love story aimed at bringing the propertied rake and servant girl together—then why bother with a novel where the sex is never really suggested but somehow always implied, when it would be easier to get the sensuous experience of things tasted and felt in a novel like *Fanny Hill*? Others said that the novel was racy despite its moral intentions, because any pretty adolescent girl who obsessively desexualizes herself brings out quite the opposite effect in her suitor and readers, kind of like stereotyped librarians or schoolmistresses do in the pornographic imagination.

As unbelievable and ironic as it may be, *Pamela* marked a shift in the history of sexual culture because, far from being a *description* of life, it prescribed a stereotype of wasp femininity that is eroding but still lingers: a pure young woman, inexperienced and delicate in physical and mental ability, who faints at the slightest hint of sexual advance. But its ideological effects didn't stop there.

In the middle-class Protestant minds of people like Richardson, sexual licence is *always* associated with the upper classes, so by denying the advances of her promiscuous rich employer, Pamela is in effect fighting the good fight against the permissiveness of an older, Catholic culture. The fact that she protects her virginity, convincing him that sex is *only* right after marriage, and then marries the guy, signals a moral victory for her salt-of-the-earth people and their domestic codes of decency.

It's just too bad that a good class war had to get all mixed up with the ideological dreck of sexual politics. Sure, it's admirable that a young girl marginalized by birth and gender can be rewarded with a better life, but are her personal virtue and inner worth the *only* things that win a reader's respect? Fanny Hill is rewarded too, but few people were as willing to admire her because instead of protecting her virginity with her life, she used her sex to get ahead. The difference between decent Pamela and self-indulgent Fanny stems from the fact that in the middle of the eighteenth century when both were written, the idea that novels were *novel* because they were about the real world gave way to a very different idea, and an altogether more heinous one. *Sensibility* and *sentiment* were now the keywords and they shifted the focus from sense to feelings, sympathy, civility, good conduct and other feel-good cultural abstractions that separate human society from the dog-eat-dog world of nature, and in the process divide people from their real passions. It's hard to say why exactly this happened, but it does have a lot to do with changes in the social and educational background of the most important writers, a lot more of whom were coming from professional families and fewer from Oxford and Cambridge.

The change in literary demographics pushed the issue of sexuality farther off the table, because just like indelicate topics are off-limits around the middle-class dining room table, so too are carnal matters improper when directly dealt with in literature. It was as the stodgy, intellectual big shot of the eighteenth century, Samuel Johnson, said: "Man's chief merit consists in resisting the impulses of nature." And sex is *the* impulse of nature, so it was the opposite of what counts as valuable in life and literature, which is emotion and the thoughtful cultivation of civility and good manners in society. A better example of this same attitude comes from Johnson's devotee, the novelist Fanny Burney, who said that although a novel should be "a picture of natural and probable human existence," whatever is "noxious or reprehensible" in it should be accompanied by what is "chastening."

From this point on, realistic novel writing—in fact *all* writing that wanted to count as literature—demanded self-censorship and veiling one's desires. It was the birth of the literary high ground and the claim that sex in literature just fills up space that could otherwise be occupied by a deep thought or social instruction. The natural functions of the human body, which up until then were seen as things that happened all the time and were fair game for novelists, were no longer fit for literary representation. Words like virtue, propriety, decency, delicacy and purity are standard fare in novels of the time and they came to have an almost exclusively prohibitive sexual connotation.

Thankfully, there were still voluptuous novels being published—lots of them. Like Laurence Sterne's *Sentimental Journey*, a story that infused schmaltzy comic characters with vigorous libidos and coded its juicy bits in highly erotic et ceteras and drop-off lines. Or the novels of Tobias Smollett, who pressed comic wordplay into the service of sexual innuendo, and Gothic novels, which poured sexualized symbolism into descriptions of hallways and bedchambers, some authors taking their cue from the sinister genius of the Marquis de Sade, a man possessed by the desire to narrate every possible erotic combination and every mode of sexual pleasure and pain.

It's not that people like Haywood and Cleland were more realistic because they were more open about sex than Richardson, Burney or the Brontë sisters, but in their writing you do sense a last gasp of liberty before novelists went trudging into the Victorian era, trenchcoats in hand and dresses hanging as low as the floor to conceal all nether regions. No new cultural form can ever stay innovative and fresh for too long before it is hijacked for ideological purposes. At the end of the eighteenth century, novels were becoming genuinely popular cultural products—especially among women readers—and that popularity meant that they were having an effect on how and what people felt, what they thought and how they acted, and about what was possible for them, if even only at the level of fiction.

In short, by the time the erectionless editors at the *Evangelical Magazine* published their little moral barometric diagram, "realism" was no longer just what happened when a novel reflected a reality existing out there; on the contrary, it was what happened when a novel concocted a version of reality that functioned well as a mollifying ideology for a new world order that didn't allow for much independent thinking, certainly not by women. That's why radicals like Mary Wollstonecraft in her political essays stressed that "the soft phrases, susceptibility of heart, and refinement of taste" hammered into women by sentimental novelists make them into "creatures of sensation" and "prevents intellect from attaining that sovereignty which it

ought to attain to." And that's why reactionaries like those evangelical editors thought up God's barometer: to warn people that
reading novels could impact their lives, not by advertising frail
refinements that turn them into dumb submissives, but by
arousing them with sex substitutes that send them to eternal
damnation. Different arguments, but prompted by the same
understanding that, far from being some creative window dressing that has no effect on reality, novels can incite and stimulate
people to do and think things.

Similes, Cigarettes and Clichés As Beautifully Worn As Maidens after a Hard Night with the Fishing Fleet

Just before Samuel L. Jackson lays down his epic "I will strike down upon thee with great vengeance" flourish in Quentin Tarantino's *Pulp Fiction*, there's a clever sequence in which his inordinately eloquent character, Jules, asks the preppy kid, Brett, who's about to be shot, to describe what Marsellus Wallace looks like. The kid's too scared to reply, so Jules asks, "Does he look like a bitch?" Stymied by the simile, the kid can only manage to say "What?" This, of course, is what Jules told him *not* to say again— answering a question with a question is never good form—so he shoots him in the shoulder and asks, with an emphasis on each syllable, "Does-he-look-like-a-bitch?" "No," the kid says. "Then why did you try to fuck 'im like a bitch?" Seconds later Jules unloads his paraphrased version of that biblical passage about charity from the Book of Ezekiel, then he and his partner Vincent—played by John Travolta—unload their pistols on him.

When the film came out in 1994—has it really been twenty-two years?—I was in grad school, where most of us liked it, though at the time we probably wouldn't admit to liking déclassé pulp fiction by Dashiell Hammett or Raymond Chandler or one of the lesser-knowns whose penny-dreadful stories appeared in cheap magazines like *Spicy Detective* or *Black Mask* in the first half of the last century. Pulp fiction is thrilling linear stories about crime, always tinged with sex, that working stiffs could carry around in their lunch pails; *Pulp Fiction* was something grad students could talk about in Derrida and Foucault seminars. Sure, the first shot in the movie features those definitions from the *American Heritage Dictionary*—"Pulp: 1. A soft, moist, shapeless mass or matter. 2. A magazine or book containing lurid subject matter and being characteristically printed on rough, unfinished paper"—but its disjointed narrative was all meta and postmodern, so self-referential that you weren't sure *what* to say about that part where, in the parking lot of Jack Rabbit Slims, the elegant Uma Thurman looks over at Travolta, who just wants to "go get a steak," and says "Don't be a…," and then breaks the fourth wall and draws a "square" right there in the camera frame but you just *knew* this was some sophisticated narratological shit. And all that playful Warholesque recycling of pop archetypes? Tarantino was ahead of his time because that kind of self-consciousness only became a compulsory cultural trope among hipsters a few years ago.

That scene where Jules delivers the rapturous passage and smokes the kid isn't memorable because of its divine violence, although that's part of it. It's memorable because the violence accentuates the importance of language in the film. The scene caps an introductory sequence in which Jules and Vincent, who are en route to an execution after the opening credits scroll by to that crisp Del-Tones' surf-rock anthem, speak reverently about Big Macs, TV pilots and the ethics of giving a married woman a foot massage. After he saw it premiere at Cannes, the film critic Roger Ebert said that it "creates a world…where breathless prose clatters down fire escapes and leaps into the dumpster of doom." It's a lovely description of the language games prominent in all pulp fiction: unencumbered characterizations, obsessively punctuation-free simple sentences and adrenaline-fuelled similes in the service of delivering entertaining content. What started out as formulaic sensationalism printed on cheap paper in tawdry magazines had morphed into a representation of those stories that treated the means of representation—the black marks on the white page—as reverentially as the content itself. I mean, seriously, does anybody even remember the significance of the one thing—that glowing briefcase those punks swiped from Marsellus—at the centre of the story?

Getting all medievally theoretical about the film might seem, to use pulp master Raymond Chandler's textbook simile from *The Long Goodbye*, "like a pearl onion on a banana split." But it's not, really, because, though it was assembly-line escapist literature produced for consumers of sublime simplicity for whom "reading" was only a guilty pleasure, pulp fiction made the stylized mechanics of everyday communication—especially, the lowly simile, poor older brother to the always more esteemed metaphor—decent and respectable, even funny at times and philosophical at others, just like the rhetoric Jules throws down at Brett before he pops him.

It was Chandler, the hard-boiled writer who invented archetypal wise-guy detective, Philip Marlowe, and whose noirish stories were made into Hollywood classics like *The Big Sleep* and *Farewell, My Lovely*, who reminded us that the simile, for all its clichéd charm and hyperbolic plainness, was, like a well-positioned carnation on the lapel of a homeless guy, quite a beautiful thing. Even the sexist ones pulsating with all that pent-up erotic energy: "Her hands dropped and jerked at something and the robe she was wearing came open and underneath it she was as naked as a September Morn but a darn sight less coy," "She bent over me again. Blood began to move around in me, like a prospective tenant looking over a house," and "She gave me a smile I could feel in my hip pocket." Similes like this, cast in the sultry ambience of a world that had yet to experience gender studies, feel scripted for a lispy Humphrey Bogart talking about the coolly insinuating Lauren Bacall.

But the appeal of Chandler's similes isn't just their wisecrack sensibility, though that has lots to do with it given that most of his Marlowe stories were rendered into popular radio dramas. Like an unexpected gust of wind cutting through a wheat field on a summer night, his narrative voice can build perceptive comparisons and make them, with minimalist syntax and rhythmic cadence, downright poetic. The blonde showgirl in *The High Window*, for example, is reclining with a glass of scotch, and Marlowe, approaching her, thinks to himself, "From thirty feet away she looked like a lot of class. From ten feet away she looked like something made up to be seen from thirty feet away." Then later in the same novel, a woman walks out of the bedroom without benefit of makeup, and Marlowe says to her, "Put some rouge on your cheeks. You look like a snow-maiden after a hard night with the fishing fleet."

Now and then that voice shifts from the pedestrian to the sublime reaches of philosophy. Here is a line from the opening chapter of *The Big Sleep*, in which Marlowe—"neat, clean, shaved, and sober, and I didn't care who knew it"—scopes out the residence of his next case: "Beyond the garage were some decorative trees trimmed as carefully as poodle dogs." Simple enough. But then, here, from the last chapter, a pared-down existentialist moment in which Marlowe, like Jean-Paul Sartre recast as a Camel-smoking private detective in a powder-blue suit, reflects on that really big question: "What did it matter where you lay once you were dead? In a dirty sump or in a marble tower on the top of a high hill? You were dead, you were sleeping the big sleep, you were not bothered by things like that. Oil and water were the same as wind and air to you." Short and plain, there's nothing in this simile to make your head hurt, though it produces a head scratcher of a thought.

Northrop Frye, the godfather of literary theory whom more people should really know about, pointed out something so obvious that it constantly needs to be pointed out, which is that figures of speech are central to all literary texts. There are two kinds of association that we use in our language as figures, he said: "Analogy and identity, two things that are like each other and two things that are each other." Similes are based on straight-up analogical thinking—this is *like* that, Marsellus is *like* a bitch, oil and water are *as* wind and air to a dead man—but metaphors are rooted in less-obvious identities. Realism in literature, Frye says, is structured like one big simile and it's at one end of the literary spectrum, the end that pulp fiction inhabits. On the other end are myth and religion, which are far richer and more meaningful in the bigger scheme of things, and they're structured implicitly on metaphor. That's why, for Frye, metaphor tells us that we desire the world to be something that it is perhaps not.

As much as I think Frye's got a point, his argument grates on my fondness for pulp fiction. Most school kids understand simile more clearly than they understand metaphor, and that's only because every simile, as every kid coming out of high school can tell you without really thinking about it, is "a comparison using like or as," whereas metaphors are less direct, more poetic. They stretch the mind a little bit more. Ludwig Wittgenstein, the Austrian genius who's credited with causing the "linguistic turn" in philosophy and who also happened to be a big reader of detective pulp fiction, once called the simile, not the metaphor, "the best thing" in philosophy. Some of our most important concepts—the stuff we call religion and ethics, for example, or aesthetics—"seem to be just similes." His point, rarely understood by people who think words are nothing but transparent pointers to a reality that exists somewhere out there independent of language, is that similes are not charming knick-knacks that adorn literal communication but are the end point of communication itself. If you can describe something by means of a simile, then you should also be able to overlook the simile and have something left. But the thing of it is, Wittgenstein noticed, there's nothing left to express if you drop the simile, because the fact *is* the simile. I'd say the same is true for metaphor: if you pull the metaphors from our core philosophies—the "invisible hand," "tabula rasa" or "box of chocolates"—then what's really left?

Look at these lines from *The Long Goodbye*, one of Chandler's last novels. Each is built on a generative simile. "Alcohol is like love. The first kiss is magic, the second is intimate, the third is routine. After that you take the girl's clothes off." If we drop the simile, what's left? Is Marlowe saying that alcohol is magic, intimate, routine and then—what?—naked, like a sexual relationship? An adolescent reader committed to the simple pleasures of canned entertainment will take the lines to mean that drinking and sex are both fun, ha ha, but when you actually *read* it you notice that the simile establishes a narrative of overpowering intoxication which you can't, ultimately, decide is a good or bad thing. And this isn't a question of "reading too much into" the lines, which we all know we're not ever supposed to do—as if reading should never develop beyond literal insignificance—but then it's not rocket science, either. I'm not sure if Wittgenstein would be tickled by Chandler's simile, but I'm pretty sure he would have agreed that the comparison—one drinks *as if* one is in love—is, like all comparisons, at the core of all literature and philosophy.

Most people, if they have any understanding of the poetic or rhetorical elements of their language, understand and use similes, and I don't just mean that youthful verbal tick of using the word "like"—which in juvenile speech is itself *like* an incomplete or fragmented simile that creates the impression of a thought happening, which of course it is—multiple times during a sentence to stand in for some elusive meaning. We use figurative language every twenty words or so when we speak and write, though if we were to deconstruct each one—even dead metaphors like "she's *cool*," "I've had a *hard* day," "this book is *deep*," and "he's a *pain in the ass*"—we'd never get stuff done. Like dead metaphors, similes are those grainy particles of language that we forget are figures of speech even though they structure our understanding of the world, those bits of language that are, like pictures of family on your mantel or like the ceilings in your house, unnoticed but necessary. And like grains of sand that float between the two shells of an oyster, some become significant on their own terms.

Writing in "The Simple Art of Murder," the 1944 *Atlantic* essay that's become a standard of pulp literary criticism, Chandler said that a good story—he was thinking of Dashiell Hammett's work—had to have "style" but that readers wouldn't know this "because it was in a language not supposed to be capable of such refinements." When people read mass-produced stories, he said, "they thought they were getting meaty melodrama, written in the kind of lingo they imagined they spoke themselves." They didn't speak this lingo, of course; they only *thought* they did, like readers today might think a story by Stephenie Meyer or George R.R. Martin is good because it's "realistic" even though that usually means the opposite because "realistic" stories like theirs, like so much original pulp fiction, leave the suspension of disbelief intact. Chandler, who was a stronger thinker than either the authors of *Twilight* or *Game of Thrones*, knew that realism is never a matter of holding up a mirror to what people do and say to one another in their real lives. Far from it. "Realism takes too much talent, too much knowledge, too much awareness," he said. The worst pulp writers, he explained, can write about a "dalliance with promiscuous blondes" with no other aim in mind "than to describe dalliance with promiscuous blondes." That pedestrian practice is little more than repetition. Good writers, though, know that "it is not a very fragrant world" but they "can make very interesting and even amusing patterns out of it." Which is where language and its similes come into the picture.

And he's right. Whether it's hard-boiled detective fiction, stories about emotionally-charged vampires or sexed-up historical fantasy, for most people the ultimate aim of reading is to do away with reading altogether and to deliver some "reality" that exists "behind" the words on the page. That's one huge artistic endeavour, no easier to pull off in pulp fiction than in more canonical literary works.

Chandler probably didn't think about similes and metaphors as obsessively as Frye or Wittgenstein, but he was more aware than most of his fellow pulp-fiction writers of the artifice that, under the constraints of mass production and consumption in the 1930s and 1940s, could finesse its way into even the most mechanical fiction. Looking back on the stories he wrote, Chandler once said, "It would be absurd if I did not wish they had been better. But if they had been much better they would not have been published. If the formula had been a little less rigid, more of the writing of that time might have survived. Some of us tried pretty hard to break out of the formula, but we usually got caught and sent back. To exceed the limits of a formula without destroying it is the dream of every magazine writer who is not a hopeless hack." I had to read that a few times before I understood that he's really talking about the necessity of finessing the linguistic principles of writing to a pedestrian point.

In the heyday of pulp fiction—1946—George Orwell wrote "The Prevention of Literature," in which he said that "low grade sensational fiction...produced by a sort of conveyor-belt process that reduces human initiative to the minimum" is a feature not of democratic but of totalitarian societies. A few years later he'd go on to satirize pulp fiction in his classic dystopian novel *1984* as ideological drivel, on par with pornography and horoscopes, "composed entirely by mechanical means" that the Ministry of Truth uses to keep people ignorant. This argument—between Orwell and the pulp writers of the 1940s, between the classist literary writers and the more populist voice of the hacks—is as old as the hills. During the summer of 2014, corporate leviathan Amazon.com, which was then engaged in an epic battle over pricing with the Hachette Book Group, invoked Orwell's old missive against the pulp writers in a letter addressed to its e-book authors and readers. You would think, Amazon pointed out with the sanctimonious rhetorical aplomb of the techno-capitalist class, that "the literary establishment of the day would have celebrated the invention of the paperback, yes?" No. Instead, there were people like Orwell who said that lowering the retail price of literature "would destroy literary culture." The Hachette Book Group, which had refused to give Amazon pricing control over its e-books, which would have seen most titles cost less than $10, was upholding the *ancien régime* of literature. Amazon, under the watchful eye of Jeff Bezos, positioned itself as a latter-day Robin Hood defending democratic values and ensuring that the sweetness and light of literary culture extended to the impoverished class of readers and writers. It waged a corporate war by asking its e-book readers and writers to email Hachette's CEO and demand that the price of e-books be lower, which is always a good selling point: "If we want a healthy reading culture, we have to work hard . . . to make books less expensive."

Anybody with a sense of literary judgment knows that a dumbing down of literature to the level of street-corner tabloid porn pulp, whether it's consumed on paper or on a screen, isn't a good thing, although it will be a cheaper thing. Chandler knew this just as well as Orwell did. The mass production of pulp, the "pooped-out piece of . . . mechanical fiction," he said, "would not be possible at all if the job took any talent." The best one can do is weave threads of artistry into that messy texture of manufactured literature, Chandler suggested, which seems exactly the right thing to do. A raucous simile here, a sultry double-entendre there, a bawdy metaphor further on. At the end of "The Simple Art of Murder" Chandler lists the qualities a good work of pulp fiction instills into its hero. There are too many to list, and all are quite typical, but none are as important as the intense faith with which Chandler wrote of this ideal type. "If there were enough like him," he said, "I think the world would be a very safe place to live in, and yet not too dull to be worth living in." Only if there were enough like him.

My Agreeable Illusion

When I was house hunting in Vancouver a few years ago I had what most people would think is a spectacularly ridiculous condition. If I was going to buy a 33' x 122' footprint, the deciding factors were going to be price (though I had good fortune to be in the market a year or two before the property values started spiralling to sublime heights) and, obviously, "location, location, location." But location didn't mean proximity to a school or Starbucks, nor did it mean neighbourhood demographics, alleyway traffic or oil tanks hidden deep in the backyard. My condition was that I wanted to live within the panoramic view novelist Ethel Wilson described in the first paragraph of her classic 1954 novel, *Swamp Angel*. And I was more or less serious, too.

I remember being met by an affably patronizing smile in the rear-view mirror when I asked the realtor, who was driving us east along Dundas Street through Vancouver Heights to the next house, if she happened to know whether it was close to where Wilson's novel opens. It's not the kind of question you should ask a highly caffeinated Vancouver real-estate agent. She knew Capitol Hill was east of the heights but she hadn't heard of Wilson, but then most Vancouverites probably don't know the name. I didn't bother telling her that I really *did* want to find a home that was inside the visual field that a writer she hadn't heard of described in a novel that is a historical mainstay of CanLit, or that it was the most evocative—and perfect—opening scene in any BC novel I'd ever read.

It's late afternoon, and Maggie Vardoe, Wilson's unsatisfied housewife protagonist, is about to walk out her back door, up the alley and into a waiting cab that will drive her away from a sterile marriage and towards a new life as a cook at an Interior fishing lodge. She's standing alone at the living-room window in her Capitol Hill home, doing what many people with pleasant views probably do when they're standing alone at a window and not talking on the phone: she looks out, surveys the panorama, and thinks.

> *Ten twenty fifty brown birds flew past the window and then a few stragglers, out of sight. A fringe of Mrs Vardoe's mind flew after them... and then was drawn back into the close fabric of her preoccupations. She looked out... over the roofs of these houses to Burrard Inlet far below, to the dark green promontory of Stanley Park, to the elegant curve of the Lions Gate Bridge which springs from the Park to the northern shore which is the base of the mountains; and to the mountains.*

Maggie, an outwardly uncomplicated Burnaby wife, just stands there and looks, but she's also canvassing the scenery like an artist would first survey a landscape. Then she has one of those moments when the ordinary things we see in our familiar environments appear ever so slightly unfamiliar to us and induce unordinary perceptions:

> *The mountains seemed, in this light, to rear themselves straight up from the shores of Burrard Inlet until they formed an escarpment along the whole length of the northern sky. The escarpment looked solid at times, but certain*

lights disclosed slope behind slope, hill beyond hill, giving an impression of the mountains which was fluid, not solid.

This is the stuff of real literature, and I can't help but think that the annual fiction prize in BC is named after Wilson because of stylistically crisp and lucid sentences like these. Her writing, vivid and unpretentious as it always is, has this graceful quality of marvel and surprise embedded in the surface of simple descriptions.

It's also the kind of writing that made me think, *yeah, it would be kind of neat if my future mortgage payments could be directed to a part of the city a fictional character looked at and thought so much about in a splendid novel.* I like how Maggie surveyed the panorama, moving her eyes along the topography from one point to the next and then hitting that wall of mountain but not quite stopping there. This way of looking at the city always seemed archetypal to me. Like an Impressionist painter who knows that objects in a landscape can't be represented accurately without considering the play of light and atmospheric conditions that enable us to see those objects in the first place, Maggie is looking at her environment with distinctly Vancouver eyes.

Looking out windows, whether in a novel or in your living room, is quite a normal activity in a visually stunning city that has a cultural fetish for voyeurism. Where else in the world does the real-estate industry, just like local literature and art, dwell on the value—both real and imagined—of points of view?

There are extraordinary views in Vancouver—most of them natural, some built, many hybrids—and the people in this city do like to look. We have what Lance Berelowitz, urban planner and author of the *2010 Olympic Winter Games* bid book, calls a "cult of view." Think of the official "view cones" city hall enshrined with their "view protection measures" to defend "view corridors" of the skyline, the North Shore and the surrounding waters from vertically obsessed developers. Or the inspired images and expressive texts city officials issue—"Vancouver's 'greenness' is overarching. It is a key to our collective identity. Vancouver citizens live in a green paradise," reads Vancouver's "Green Capital" brand promotion—to inculcate a sublime sense of civic optics for its citizens and potential investors.

I certainly bought into the cult of the Vancouver *trompe l'œil*—metaphorically but also financially—even though only three of the city's twenty-seven designated "view cones" are in East Van—Main Street, Commercial Drive, Trout Lake—and none of them protect what I see when I look up from this screen and out the window of my Hastings-Sunrise home and survey pretty much the same panorama Maggie does in Wilson's novel.

In no other city does the literature, even the bureaucratic literature produced by civic officials and realtors, fixate on the natural and urban geography as in Vancouver. Pauline Johnson's mythical Lions peaks, Douglas Coupland's city of glass, Zsuzsi Gartner's perpetually beckoning city of land and sea, Malcolm Lowry's contemptuous mountains gazing down on infernal Hastings Street, Sky Lee's historically pungent Chinatown. And Wilson's Capitol Hill, which I think is the most ample point of view from which to look at Vancouver precisely because it is *not* one of the more clichéd vantage points—southern, northern, western—from which the city tends to be depicted in photography and tourist trinketry. Close enough to downtown—Maggie Vardoe walked there—but a bit of an innocuous and remote asymmetrical mound of sandstone in north Burnaby, Capitol Hill is bisected with working- and middle-class residential streets, enclosed at its base by East

Hastings, a city park and a sprawling refinery. It's entirely average, except for its comprehensive view.

In Wilson's short story "A Drink with Adolphus," Mrs. Gormley tells her daughter that she needs to get to Capitol Hill by taxi to visit her friend. "To see the view. The house is old but he's mad about the view on Capitol Hill." And in "The Window," a character, Mr. Willy, has a window on the north-west wall of his home that looks out over the water and mountains, just like Maggie does in *Swamp Angel*. The view is nice, but Wilson says the mountains are "deceptive in their innocency, full of crags and crevasses and arêtes and dangers." In literature as in life what we see when we look at things is never exactly what is literally there. I've looked out my window thousands of times since I moved into Wilson's literary panorama. It never *really* changes, neither in shape nor the throb of its volume, but like an optical illusion where a static object looks to be always in motion, the scene always *is* different, and I'm not just talking about the giant wind turbine that somebody stuck up on Grouse Mountain.

I imagine that when creative types look at a landscape, they see those shifts all the time. BC's beloved Emily Carr, who spent an awful lot of time staring at trees and mountains and then painting them, said that when she looked she saw "there was a coming and going among trees, that there was sunlight in shadows." As for Wilson, she was a painterly writer with a talent for wrapping her words around the rippling facade in scenery. In a talk she once gave to the *BC Society of Artists*, she mentioned taking lessons from Carr at her Granville Street studio early in the last century.

Reality, whether it's in a novel or framed by your living-room window, involves empirical objects like trees and mountains, but these objects in their composition often express something ethereal, like those vibrations and mysterious undercurrents pulsating just beneath the surface. What Maggie sees is a defamiliarized inventory of Vancouver landmarks that are familiar to anybody who lives here. The crows that gather every late afternoon and commute in those swirly, undulating diagonal sky paths from across the Lower Mainland to roost in that unlikely forest by Still Creek and Willingdon Avenue. The massive thumbprint of Stanley Park. The harbour. Lions Gate and the ubiquitous North Shore, where those mountains really do look like a flat green-black stage background until your eyes register colour and depth, consider the variations in the light and its textured effect on the landscape, and then slowly notice the range of gradations and the separate hills that give the backdrop depth and dimension and make it look "fluid."

Maggie isn't looking at a static high-res image. The focal point that dominates the panorama—the *punctum* that "pierces the viewer" as the French semiotician Roland Barthes puts it—is not one object in the inert landscape but the light and its fluid effect on the land. Like any Vancouverite who looks north, her eyes just stop at that 100-million-year-old granite and metamorphic rock of the Coastal Mountains, which at first look like a wall with height and width but then take on a third dimension, with a foreground that somehow recedes farther and farther back. That optical phenomenon is probably the closest thing Vancouver has to an official way of seeing, which has less to do with passively apprehending the reality we see "out there" and more to do with our desire to give that reality a sense of meaning, structure and purpose by stylizing it as a fictional entity.

A little later, after she gets into that cab and leaves her house and husband on Capitol Hill, Maggie is driving through the "drenched sameness" of East Van. Down by the Fraser River she notices that the houses and roads on the south slope are in an "agreeable illusion." They are on the edge of urban sprawl, but they *look* pastoral and remote. Wilson calls it that "intrinsic quality of appearing to be far removed from a city," which is the dream of any green-minded civic politician. But that natural landscape is always distorted by what Maggie recognizes as "the amenities of living, learning, playing, and dying." That's Maggie's last visual impression of Vancouver in Wilson's 1954 novel: a city intent on an "agreeable illusion" that melts development into the fabric of its landscape. We're not talking about Vancouverites recycling their herbal-tea sachets or overusing adjectives like "sustainable" to enact some eco-spiritual at-one-ness with their environment. It's more like a need to pull meaning from that bulky panorama we're always looking at, to leave a footprint—though perhaps not an ugly carbon footprint—on the natural geography so we know that we're here and that we *mean*.

A few months ago I was looking for images from local artists—from Carr and Frederick Varley to Tiko Kerr and Luciana Alvarez—to show in my Vancouver Lit class. I was surprised to find that painter Laura Zerebeski had just finished a piece called *Capitol Hill*—currently on show at the Beaumont Gallery. Zerebeski's popular Vancouver paintings—one of them was used as promotion for The Drift/Art on Main Street weekend art tour in 2009—distort recognizable landmarks in the built environment, not to the point of full abstraction but only so those familiar reference points appear wobbly and fluid, as if they've been underpainted with an electrically charged glaze that ignites the composition from the inside, making it appear to writhe and ripple with currents of vibrant energy.

She calls her work "exuberantly satirical landscapes" and says they generate a "whimsical" view of the place. And they do. *Capitol Hill* is driven by a delightfully fierce energy of observation. It's a warm and wiggly painting with a shimmery niceness that at first glance might look like commemorative tourist art to people who prefer the more cerebral message of abstract art. What struck me about *Capitol Hill*—apart from the fact that it's from the same vantage point as the panorama in Wilson's novel—is that it liquefies Vancouver's decipherable geography into a pleasant—but not absurdly syrupy—cartoon-like expression. This is the kind of painting that I'd want hanging on a wall in my house with a good view. Zerebeski paints like an Expressionist with a fondness for Edvard Munch and the Group of Seven, and a penchant for DC Comics—say, the round active swirls, soft lines and feminine curves of Wonder Woman.

The surface texture in *Capitol Hill* is coolly euphoric. The curling lines and bold colours are sensual, as if the cloud formations in that vital sky were painted by a supple finger. The rimpled mountains and hill formations, which sometimes resemble human bodies in profile, as well as the greenery are rhythmic and heavily drenched in strong colours, though they're not quite as pulsating as they are in a typical Emily Carr forest. That undulating beam of light extending out from beneath the Ironworkers, across the harbour and past the Lions Gate to a vanishing point beyond English Bay, might anchor our view because it's central, but the more you look at it the more it appears supplemental to the green and blue of the prevailing geography.

"Like a piece of ice on a hot stove," poet Robert Frost once said, a poem "must ride on its own melting," and the same applies to Zerebeski's painting. There are no people in *Capitol Hill* but everything in it—mountains, water, bridges, the sky—looks like it's moving of its own volition. The northern slope of residential streets in Vancouver Heights and the southern footings of the bridges. The harbour—a single ship at anchor—framed by a darkened Stanley Park and a slightly menacing darker harbour just north of East Van, and the busy clutter of portside on the North Van shore. Even those two ubiquitous sulphur piles—as visually distinct here as pyramids in Egypt—and the Lions Gate Bridge. The mountains at the western tip of the North Shore and then the Sunshine Coast.

If there is a meaning in this painting, a purpose beyond its own picturesque beauty, I think it must be in the convergence of the natural and built environments. The black hull of the cargo ship is indistinguishable from the phantasmic caerulean blue water, which then becomes turquoise and then elides into the greens of the shoreline. Even the three bridges, the most unnatural objects in the frame, yield seamlessly from their unseen junctions with the landscape. The trussed spans and the arches, as well as the contours of the buildings on the North Shore, are not in contrast to the land formation but mirror it. Every built form finds an echo elsewhere—its texture in the water and sky, its shape in the mountains.

Zerebeski's *Coal Harbour Panorama* (2008) is a slightly better example of this echo effect. The houses in West Van and the bridge are barely noticeable, and the buildings along the North Shore mirror in their contours the mountains behind them. It's a more typical work because it is a much more common vantage point—the chic Pan Pacific Hotel—and a more idealized view, too, because it doesn't include the noisy port activity of *Capitol Hill*. This work is in line with the great tradition of an idyllic, heavily romanticized landscape in BC. Although this is a more traditionally attractive work—only a giclee print is on show— there is a more attentive and realistic pattern in *Capitol Hill*, a kind of gestalt that illustrates a struggle between industry and natural landscape without rendering the necessary fact of urban living into a romantic celebration of a city's sacred harmony with nature. The built geography mirrors the natural geography, but it's also outsized and—far more importantly—outsignified by it. Sort of like that "agreeable illusion" Wilson writes about, *Capitol Hill* represents a distinctly Vancouver structure of feeling—or seeing—where the fluidity of vision makes everything in the panorama go parallel with the more comprehensive shape of the mountains and subtly throbbing textures of air and water.

I'm not sure if Zerebeski's work is at all indebted to the work of Carr, but I think it must be. A lot of Carr's later work was composed in those swirling brushstrokes that she pulled from the Expressionists. And like the Group of Seven, Carr made the brushstroke itself a central component of her work, and that emphasis on the material itself—the movement and method of the actual composition—is distinct in *Capitol Hill*, where the built environment is artificially made to melt into its natural context but without losing its distinction from it. Zerebeski once said in an interview "everything around me—trees, water, mountains, buildings— seemed to have brushstrokes," which to me sounds like how a painter conceptualizes the texture of form that can make landscape fluid. If Wilson is a painterly writer, then Zerebeski is certainly a textual artist.

A painting is meant to hang on a wall and be looked at and

considered, not just to be squeezed onto a shelf or to invade a reader's mind and make him want to buy a house in a very specific location of a city. I'd put *Capitol Hill* on a wall in my house, right across the shelf from where *Swamp Angel* sits, if there weren't another shelf there already. Not for any mysterious reasons. They both seem just so appropriate for living here because between the built and natural elements in their landscapes, and in our panoramas, we can feel our own lives suspended.

Wordsworth on Grouse Mountain

In the neighbourhood of latitude fifty north, and for the last
hundred years or thereabouts, it has been an axiom that
Nature is divine and morally uplifting.

—"Wordsworth in the Tropics," Aldous Huxley

They looked like people who should have been in an art gallery.
The two men were dressed in black—one in a Prada jumper
and the other with a mandarin collar—though it was June and
warm. Prada wore rectangular black-framed glasses iconic of the
urban property-owning professional set. The two women were
in yoga wear more indicative of an excess of leisure time than
stretching and sweating. They were eating lunch, looking out of
the windows over the Lower Mainland, and talking about
home—somewhere around Chicago—but every so often one of
them would make one of those characteristically hyperbolic
tourist affirmations that require no response except other affirmations. *What a beautiful view. Is Stanley Park ever big. Look how
green everything is. It smells like camping here.*

It was charming, listening to their innocuous rhetorical praises
of Vancouver from the next table, where I sat with my own
tourist—a niece visiting from London, Ontario, who had begged
me to take her to "do the Grind." She had heard about it from a
friend who had been out here and done it, decided it couldn't be
that hard when I pointed out Grouse Mountain when we were
driving back from the airport that morning and told her it was
three kilometres long and 3000 feet up, and she even managed

to make it up later that afternoon, wheezing and inconspicuosly cursing and fuming at the experience like only a precocious fourteen-year-old girl can curse and fume at experiences that can't talk back for the hour and a half she trailed behind me.

She hated it, but of course when we were sitting there in the cafeteria next to the tourists at the top, she assured me that "no, it wasn't *that* hard," and then, after I told her that this "Grind" is a walk in the park for a lot of locals and that it even has its own Facebook page, she said she didn't care and would never do it again even if she lived here. *Why would she ever want or need to do it again when she just proved she can do it? That would be stupid.* She didn't seem to notice when the Prada fella launched into an impromptu poetic reverie about the slices of low-level clouds pushed up against the trees and how "mystical" this made the atmospheric perspective. *Mystical.* It sounded so very important when he said it, especially compared to the words coming out of my lovely niece's mouth. Sitting there, between my complaining neice and the praising tourists, I wondered what someone like Burke or Kant would say about our experiences of nature. Kant, for one, said that the feeling associated with the sublime can be a feeling of pleasure and displeasure. Nature can inspire genuine awe, in which case we are mesmerized by its power, or it can inspire displeasure, a physical powerlessness in the face of its strength. Kind of like how Prada and his friends seemed so convinced that that was no ordinary skyride to an ordinary mountain at the far northern edge of an ordinary coastal suburb—no, this mountain has a soul and had to be talked about in metaphysical language—and how my lovely niece thought it was a pain in the ass, but did it anyways.

A hiking friend of mine who also happens to be an English

professor uses the phrase "Wordsworth bungles" when, in the course of one of our mystical hiking excursions, we encounter a problem. He came up with the phrase from an obscure 1929 essay by Aldous Huxley, who debunked the Romantic poet Wordsworth's near-mythical belief that Nature is pretty much benign, beautiful and inspirational, just like he found it appeared to be in well-gardened England in the 1820s. Once, on the way back from a long hike up to The Lions peaks to get that view of Vancouver, he fell and gashed his ankle on some rocks. Another time, when we were hiking up behind Mount Seymour, he fell and cut his leg on a sharp extrusion of pine. Those are events that he calls Wordsworth bungles. Basically, they occur when our romantic idealizations of "Nature," whether in poems or tourist brochures, run up against the inconvenient unidealized reality of sharp rocks, pine branches, trees bugs, bears and long hikes back down.

Naturally, I didn't say anything to show up Prada's touristical imitations of Wordsworth. When in the summer after a hike I linger at the top of Grouse or any of the other more easily accessible mountains longer than any local really should and find myself among visitors, especially foreigners, who pay to get up there, I tend to feel self-consciously superior. "Yeah, I just walked up here," I feel like saying, "and it wasn't even *that* hard." As much as I know that visitors like Prada who come from the bigger, flatter and oceanless cities make all kinds of hyperbolic claims about Vancouver that can be demystified with minimum effort, there is a part of me that likes hearing these little tourist fictions because I have managed to hallucinate that by some nearly Freudian transference they *must* reflect on me, too.

I thought of Prada and his Wordsworth moment of tourist

sublimity a few weeks later when a colleague sent me the weblink to a draft proposal to have Vancouver designated a "World City of Literature" by UNESCO. The organizers behind the initiative—a group led by the founding director of the Vancouver Writers Fest—submitted this stirring dossier to UNESCO's Creative Cities Network, whose mandate, as far as I can tell, is to give cities "with established creative pedigrees" the opportunity to "share experiences and create new opportunities ... notably for activities based on the notion of creative tourism." The splashy, organic rhetoric was not just aimed at getting more tourists to come and spend their money here, in other words; it's about getting smarter and creative ones—perhaps richer, foreign ones like Prada?—to come and plant some economic roots here, and hopefully create the conditions of possibility for further "creative" investment. It was the literary sublime harnessed for economic awesomeness.

In 2009, one year before the Winter Olympics arrived here, Vancouver applied for the designation "City of Literature"—other cities applied for categories like film, folk art, gastronomy and so on—and was in competition with Amsterdam, Alexandria and Krakow for the honour of having this noble brand confered. The dossier, a fetching fifty-seven pages put together by Turner-Riggs Strategy Marketing Communications, brims with positive information about BC's literary history and culture. As readable and pleasing to the touch as a Denny's breakfast menu, the document aims to show the people at UNESCO headquarters in Paris that Vancouver, to which the marketing lyricists assign the twin monikers "the Natural City" and "the Literary City," is "ready to reach out and contribute to the global literary community by becoming a World City of Literature."

I realize that documents like this—if the genre had a name it should be called the *administrative sublime*—are meant to be ratified without having been read, *not* read and certainly not thought about. But I can't help think that a proposal to have a city designated as "literary" by the global authority that hands out these honours really should count on having some "literary" criticism fired at it, given that "Literature"—if it has anything useful to offer the world, besides tourism—teaches us about the many wonderful and wonderfully shifty things that can be done with words and sentences.

So how, I wonder, should we read sentences that declare there is a "buzz, energy, and excitement" in Vancouver's cultural scene, or that its literary community is "characterized by an openness to experimentation, a plurality of voices, and a mingling of cultures and traditions"? It's awfully pretty to think so, of course, but has it ever been literally true in a city like this? And how do we decode the many, many sentences in the dossier that boldly claim that Vancouver's natural geography is vital to its literary lifeblood—"Its stunning natural environment of mountains, coast, and sea inspires local and visiting artists and writers"—as if all that's needed for literature to happen in a place is a metaphyisical conjunction of water, a rapid shift in elevation and trees?

Did the writers intend that this document be read literally, or is this a little bit of metaphorical public relations poetry that needs to be read allegorically with the broadest possible interpretive arc and with an even broader nod to the real economic imperatives for which it is a euphemism? Or are they performative sentences that don't really describe anything that exists "out there" in real Vancouver at all but rather intend to produce the things they describe just by describing them that way?

I have no idea. Texts like this, which are as theologically driven as the Bible and as arousing as pornography, leave me linguistically bafflegabbed and cognitively flummoxed, much like the provincial government's pre-2010 PR mantra: *"British Columbia: The Best Place on Earth."* What kind of narcissistic delusion is *that*, anyways?

The only thing I can say for sure is that reading the UNESCO proposal requires a *willing suspension of disbelief* greater than any I have ever mustered when reading *any* literary text, Wordsworth's poetic venerations of daffodils and surrealist novels included. I imagine some purists getting hold of the document—especially if the Vancouver proposal wins—and pointing out that it marks a further erosion of literary culture in our late-capitalist era, and they may have a point because the mark of the postmodern phase of capitalism is the full conflation of economics with culture.

The text imagines a cultural makeover in which the orthodox definition of "Literature" as a field that is always at odds with "Economics," at least nominally, morphs into just another consumer item—in this case, a catalyst for tourism and future investment and speculation. Take Vancouver's literary scene, toss in vague ideological mystifications about its super-natural natural environment, and you're left with intelligent "bling" for the global creative class, which may be only a euphemism for rich property owners and property developers.

And yet, the proposal is less an imaginative makeover than a statement of the obvious, isn't it? I mean, really, whoever still thinks Literature is a sacred object set apart from consumerism and the laws of supply and demand just hasn't caught on to the fact that what counts as culture is a lot more than the books and magazines that only a handful of bright people read. Maybe the "World City of Literature" proposal is a work of unusual genius because, in its shameless romanticization of Vancouver as the "natural" and "literary" city, it has managed to understand that consumerism *is* our daily culture, right on par with sushi, jogging and trips to Grouse Mountain.

And maybe that's what we want to think of ourselves, too. Just like the view from Grouse Mountain has everything to do with idealizing the city and very little to do with the actually existing nature that can hurt and be hard to hike through, the proposal presents us with an image of our ego-ideal. It's not about how we *really* live—not exactly—but about how we would like to be seen by others, as likeable and liveable. And literary.

Poetry Isn't Elsewhere: Vancouver Poetry

A couple of years ago Stan Persky, the closest thing Vancouver has to a public intellectual, wrote that "the disappearance of poetry from public view" is like "losing a way of understanding something about life that we don't get from other linguistic modes, such as story, discourse or the language of science." He said this in a review of George Stanley's book-length poem, *Vancouver: A Poem*, which was all but ignored in the local press.

Poetry has only ever managed to blip on the public's likeability radar in fits and starts—in Skittles jingles, when Don Draper in *Mad Men* recites a Frank O'Hara stanza and Amazon.com sells out of the book, or when city hall puts out a call for applications to be Vancouver's next poet laureate. More poetry is probably read in schools than anywhere else, and if you get paid to teach poetry, then part of your job is selling it to students who think poetry is unusually complicated writing by introverts and narcissists obsessed with producing cryptic lines that don't go all the way to the end of the page. Or they just think that poetry is writing that happens elsewhere, like in Europe or in another century.

One way to sell poetry is to persuade them that poetry can be enigmatic and discreet, sexy and even complicated—in the philosophic, not Facebook, way—and that it's the only kind of writing they'll ever experience that can drill its way into the thought control centre of their minds and deposit a load of knowledge there. And that it can happen right here.

Here are lines from "Vancouver Lights," a poem Earle Birney wrote in the middle of wwii. It's about the smallness of humanity, represented in the way the city's lights look against the dark backdrop of mountains.

> We are a spark beleaguered
> by darkness   this twinkle we make in a corner of
>   emptiness [...]
> Yet we must speak   we the unique glowworms [...]
>   These rays were ours
> We made and unmade them

This is not, I say, an emo maze of words; it's a vodka-enhanced Red Bull of philosophical insight and it happened right here at Spanish Banks, not in a Paris café. We label it with "garrison mentality" or some other CanLit cliché, but the lines mean that places—like Vancouver—don't speak; we—the "glowworms" who live here—speak for them. And that's a distilled shot of pure existential lyricism.

Here are lines from "Pacific Door," Birney's poem about the early explorers who were sailing in the waters off Vancouver, looking for the Northwest Passage:

> Come then on the waves of desire that well forever
> and think no more than you must
> of the simple unhuman truth of this emptiness

The history of BC isn't sexy, and knowing lines like this isn't going to make people like you, I tell students, but there's a sensuality in knowing a nicely cut cluster of words about how we mythologize desire. Drake, Cook and the Spaniards found something "unhuman" when they were on their boats looking at Vancouver before it was Vancouver: "waves of desire" brought them here, not just some textbook impulse of political or economic conquest.

Like some people's online relationship status, poetry is "complicated," so sometimes I've even said that a poem is like a cleavage barely glimpsed beneath taffeta or a busted-up leather jacket that smells like cigarettes and sweat but which is nonetheless alluring. This is from George Bowering's eroticized account of how Captain Vancouver met up with the Spanish explorer, Quadra, just off the coast here:

> The soft air of the inland sea
> & heaving spray in the dark spruce
> offer no grail, it was no grail
> he was after, he was not
> sailing with that kind of purity.

That's a lodestar of artful candour in the space of a tweet. Like the stylized crescendo of erotica, its appeal isn't obvious: Vancouver's impure search was a kind of sexual appetite, not a simple quest for a better trade route. Think about *that* next time you're at 12th and Cambie and see the statue of the periwigged man pointing.

Like Bowering's explorer, a poet isn't a discoverer but a maker—of stories, myths, knowledge—who makes thought ingots out of words. Sometimes they're about specific places. Stand at the Carnegie Centre and look up Main to the mountains and think of Malcolm Lowry's sonnet, "Christ Walks in This

Infernal District Too." It's a little bit of literary tourism, sure, but it does look like "the mountains gaze in absolute contempt" on the Downtown Eastside. Or think of Michael Turner's collection *Kingsway* next time you're driving out to Metrotown, and you just might notice how his experiment with structure modulates with the weirdness of that nonsensical diagonal street.

Poems are like discourses in that, like philosophy, they contain knowledge but their focus isn't just on delivering some knowledge but also on how we get to that knowledge in that word engine. Even when they're *about* Vancouver, all poems are really about doing things with language. Like when Heather Haley, who has the sexiest voice in all of poetry, puts a contemporary spin on that historical desire to make a culture out of Nature in her poem "Habitat": "We plan like architects to bring the outdoors/in." It's the sheer simplicity of the lines, perforated with that little line break, that produces the thought.

Look at Chris Hutchinson's "The Man Who Lives in the Gazebo," a poem about a homeless guy in this "ineloquent metropolis." People going to work "step around him, living shadows, unrepentant/in their trespass," while Vancouver, our "ineloquent metropolis"

> clears its throat but never speaks—as language
> is held within us as we sleep, words
> whose meanings fold in on themselves—
> on waking, shut the door.

Knowing these lines might compel you to not pretend to *not* see the homeless person you walk by. Or it might implant that vexing question—if Vancouver spoke what would it say?—in your mind, where you'll toss it around and consider it just because you have a mind that is capable of considering big questions.

Poetry, Aristotle said, is finer than history because it deals with universals not particulars. Think about that when you're figuring out the meaning of "Thirteen Ways of Looking at a Gray Whale," Brad Cran's poem about those two gray whales that swam into English Bay in 2011:

> And there you were
> below the mountains
> in the heart of the city
> gazing at the gray whale.
> *You must change your life.*

That whale, like that blackbird in Wallace Stevens's poem, is a paean to the subtle epiphanies you'd never learn about in philosophy. A poem is a thought ingot you carry around in some corner of your head, and every once in a while some situation or person—maybe the way that a whale looks in the bay or maybe just the way the wind smells at Hastings and Commercial or how the sun hits the Skytrain at Science World—will make you pull a line out and say it to yourself or give it to somebody else.

Vancouver poet Catherine Owen once said poetry "is language, whether spoken or written or preferably both and [it] cannot truly become something it is not at its core." She was saying something that philosophers, and people like Persky, have been saying for ages and have to keep saying because people need to be reminded: it's not us who speak language, it's language that speaks us. It structures everything about us: our sense of time and space, our relationships and our selves, and obviously our sense of place, too.

That's what poets seem to know and, as far as I can tell, keep trying to remind us. That's what poetry is for.

The View from Zero Avenue

Becoming America

If you drive south from Vancouver you'll eventually get to Zero Avenue, which is a perfectly average residential road. Canada ends and America begins a few metres from the southern edge of Zero Avenue, where the shoulder slopes into a shallow ditch, some bushes, the occasional fence and footpath, but not much else. For a typical suburban street, Zero Avenue feels weird. It's so close that if you rolled down your window and spit out your gum, it would land in America. Or if you crushed a beer can and threw it south, it could hit an American porch or back window.

That narrow strip of no man's land at the border always makes me think bizarre thoughts about the particulars of international relations. What if some Canadian kids were playing hockey, and their ball bounced over to the American side? Could they go get it or would they have to wait until someone threw it back? Could it be thrown back without a customs slip? If that ball hit an American car and dented the hood, how would the issue get resolved? Would it be considered an attack on America?

Loopy symbolism. The houses on the Canadian side face south, as do the houses on the American side, so does that mean we're in America's backyard, and that they are, in every way that matters, more of a front-line country with a far better view on what's really going on in the 'hood? Do we look to America, and does America look to itself? And the road is called Zero Avenue, so does this suggest a kind of metaphorical nothingness? It seems to, especially when you compare it to the road the American houses face, which is called A Street, as if their side of the border were not an end but the first stage in a huge lexicon.

It is both fascinating and appalling being so close to a country that is so beautifully open in its unsophisticated arrogance that, for years, it practiced an unnerving unilateralism—in legal, environmental, economic and military issues—while it was telling everybody else we were living in one world, ready or not. How do they pull off that shit-kicking button-down marine-corps egoism? All those freedom-loving people ready to be heroes and fight the good fight against bad people but, by God, never willing to take no crap from no one.

From our side of the road, it's so perfectly disturbing, and so disturbingly mesmerizing because it's so awesome. Apart from hating them, which is easy enough for any rational-minded person living in the world today, we try to be like them and to be liked by them.

There was nothing worse than the juvenile heart flutter that lots of people in this country felt when President George Bush didn't mention "Canada" in that first rally-the-troops speech he made in September 2001. It has all the poise of a fourteen-year-old girl with braces asking around to find out if that fine-looking jock in her class had ever mentioned her by name. And then, after he mentioned us a couple of days later, while he was saying that he really needed our help in this latest foreign-policy adventure, some people whined that America was pushing a nationalist agenda on the rest of the world. Which it was. But then we got into our own patriotic titter and, thinking that we could really matter in the world too, we sent ships to the Arabian Sea to fight against a landlocked country. And our right-wing people started salivating whenever they heard someone talk about a security perimeter around the continent, either because it would keep our enemies out or because in some profoundly existential way they want to be more like the men down there.

A few days after the war started, Dalton Camp, one of this country's last Red Tories, said that the government was plunging the country "into a war whose cause it does not even have a rudimentary knowledge of, and into an alliance with a foreign government for whom it has a desperate, uncritical need to please." An uncritical need to please. And, like a scrawny kid tagging along with his older brother, we could show them that we have what it takes to play with the big boys. So for a few days in October every important Canadian minister—defence, finance, foreign affairs—said this country could "punch above its weight," and the more you heard it, the more it sounded like the Cowardly Lion jumping out at Dorothy and the Scarecrow, saying, "Put 'em up, put 'em up."

America

They say that people started reading more books after September 11, fishing around for answers, no doubt, in a damaged world. I came across this confession by New York City novelist Nat Hentoff in one of the books I picked up: "Our foreign policies will lead us into an increasing neo-imperialist role. The cant will be different from that of nineteenth-century imperialists—though not all that different—but the result will be persistent attempts to manage the political and economic directions of the underdeveloped countries. In this conflict . . . there will be more killing. And the unthinkable will be increasingly possible."

Today, most New York City writers would be less cynical, more openly upbeat, about their country, but this was written before the unthinkable happened. It's from a 1967 issue of *Partisan Review*. Someone was doing a fall cleaning. I found it in a box of their stained discards.

Maybe it's true that today we read everything through the degrading lens of September 11, perhaps even to ridiculous levels. But I couldn't help thinking that Hentoff was pulling a Nostradamus and giving his fellow New Yorkers thirty-four years warning to leave the city.

In 1967, while we were having a go at restrained jingoism up here, America was pretending that it really wasn't doing all those horrible things in Vietnam. But at least the *Partisan Review* had the balls to ask the always-important question: "What is Happening to America?" At least back then there was something besides ultrapatriotic requiems and "America-can-do-no-wrong" rhetoric rising from the chorus of political ideas. At least some people believed that America should be relying more on the force of example than the force of guns when playing its role as the world's imperial magistrate. At least they were willing to tell the American public that it was high time they understood that their super-sized empire plays such a dominant role in world history— more influential than the Roman or Byzantine, more powerful than the British—that people in other parts of the world were bound to get pissed off every once in a while.

Like the owner of that box of books, today America is cleaning house and throwing out its sense of being "in history." It's not good form, not right now, to feel anything except justified horror, let alone let memory probe anywhere beyond that soul-deadening image of two fully fuelled jet liners punching holes into the twin towers of the World Trade Center (WTC).

The Crusades, colonial dependency, the creation of an Israeli state, the overbearing need for oil, funding for anti-communist mujahideen fighters, embargoed Iraqis, bombed pharmaceutical workers in Khartoum, the octopus reach of American cultural capital, intifada, the political immaturity and potential wickedness of a humiliated people led by retrograde mullahs, the media savvy of religious freaks who timed the second collision so it could be filmed by the cameras still shooting the first hit: material history and concrete networks of interest pushed aside by muscular abstractions like Evil, Liberty and Justice, and trumped by a messianic militarism that is at once different from but similar to that ruthless divine impulse that led those lunatics with their box cutters to the cockpit doors.

The Age of Terror

Jules Michelet, the French historian, who probably should have been a poet, spent a lot of time wondering how to record the rhythm and tempo of big world events in his books. When he sat down to write about the Great Terror, that gruesome episode of political purging by guillotine just after the French Revolution, there was an insufferable intensity in his words. The contracting atmosphere of the age, the moral panic, the fragmented horror of all those heads sliced from their bodies—all of it required a different style of writing. "No more big chapters," Michelet said, "but little sections, speeding by one after the other. The prodigious acceleration of pulse is the dominant phenomenon of the Terror."

The same could be said of any age of terror. Or "Terrorism."

For all the prissy sociological claims that every violent act is triggered by a vital cause, terrorism is just a spontaneous act. It sends a message, but are the messengers motivated by a political program? Take a bunch of poor testosterone-loaded adolescent boys, enroll them in madrasa, stick a Koran in front of them, teach them to read beyond its poetry and seize on the subordinate clauses that justify apocalyptic violence, and they will suppose that the fast track to paradise is an act of consecrated suicide. Like a supreme egoist pretending that his every move has extraterrestrial significance, killing an infidel is inspired by a hubris of the will. It absolves you—and only you—from due process on judgment day.

And then the fragments in the aftermath. High tension and a crisis in the Western nervous system, layoffs and increased chocolate sales, a run on Cipro and antidepressants, paranoia at the mailbox, more people having sex and going to church, empty lineups at the airports, the supposed death of irony and humour, countries that matter securing their borders and countries that don't wondering if they should squeeze in, omnibus security measures coming down faster than the American president can say "Freedom itself was attacked this morning by a faceless coward." We may be feeling the pressure of social and political conflicts, but we are not living through history, not if by this word we mean having a sense of what just happened.

Very little time—and, with the exception of the Al Jazeera TV network, little critical dialogue—took place between the act, the accusation and the punishment. When the history of this period is told, Michelet might say, its writers will use non sequiturs and sentence fragments to imitate the speed with which "America under Attack" shifted into "The War against Terrorism" and an act motivated by "faceless" attackers became state terrorism sponsored by a pathetic sandbox of a country.

But there is this difference. For Michelet, the point was to use the words to match the event. Today, events are made to happen for the sake of words. Just after the attack, even before that Central Asian warlord's face became the stock symbol of all that was bitter and dark in the world, the U.S. and its media people started saying that this was a mission of monumental Good against monumental Evil. And the president, with all the aplomb an angry Texan can muster, and like his father before him with those other flaming Islamists in Iraq, was telling the world "there will be no negotiation."

And just as his military people were making chinks in Taliban country, he stood in front of the United Nations and said to the world that America "did not ask for this mission" but now it had "a chance to write the story of our times, a story of courage defeating cruelty and light overcoming darkness."

He kept his word. There was no negotiation. America wrote the story and followed the script. And when the bombs dropped on the 100 civilians in the village of Chowkar-Karez, a Pentagon official told CNN that it was "a fully legitimate target" because it was a centre of Taliban activity: "The people there are dead because we wanted them dead."

Virtual War

Americans live like the beleaguered inhabitants of an encircled town whose capacity for moral and ethical judgment is in inverse proportion to its gunpowder reserves. They are arrogant, yes, but more importantly they suffer from an obsessive forgetting that the potential for political violence is how things often get done—from throwing tea overboard in Boston Harbor to over-throwing the apartheid regime in South Africa—and that it doesn't really matter if those events have a progressive or reactionary bent. And this forgetting happens despite the fact that everyone knows that American governments have sponsored acts of violence when it is in their best interests.

What passes for political truth is that terrorism is always an exception. People seem to believe that the religious terrorist is an uncivilized fanatic—which he certainly is—acting out of a mad desire for martyrdom, a barbaric lust for revenge, or for some bizarre conception of the greater good. And that this sort of behaviour is un-American.

But this is forgetting that war and violence are sacraments in America. That the men who have died for Old Glory are honoured with military awards, that the bloodlust in the U.S. was more acute after September 11 than ever before, and that martyrdom is certainly not a mannerism exclusive to uncivilized Islamists.

Thus in his presidential address of October 7, George W. Bush rallied the troops with this powerfully childish anecdote: "I recently received a touching letter that says a lot about the state of America in these difficult times—a letter from a fourth-grade girl, with a father in the military: 'As much as I don't want my Dad to fight,' she wrote, 'I'm willing to give him to you.'"

The Last Irony

Whatever happened to Pennsylvania? That field where the third plane crashed doesn't amount to a hill of beans in the symbolic order of importance. Apart from deaths, the seriousness of a terrorist act is measured by the magnitude of its capacity for metaphorical destruction: first the Twin Towers, then the Pentagon; first the financial and then the military capital. Pennsylvania doesn't compare.

After the towers collapsed, America was discombobulated. Understandably so. Its nuclear power stations were sealed off, airline travel was suspended, military men were posted on subways and in train stations; but other parts of America's critical infrastructure were secured, too, like the Liberty Bell and Disneyland. Lots of people have fished around for a big theory, a catchy image or philosophical sound bite that nobody else has thought of to explain what happened on September 11. A cultural theorist named Slavoj Žižek came up with this explanation: if there is any symbolic meaning in the New York attack, it is "the notion that the two WTC towers stood for the centre of virtual capitalism, of financial speculations disconnected from the sphere of material production."

The idea here is that the terrorists gave the world a rude wake-up call by showing that, despite ten years of fatuous globalization talk, there is a huge difference—in wealth, in power, in influence—between the real Third World and immaculate America. The WTC mattered most not because it was a workplace where thirty-four-year-old guys found well-paying jobs at Cantor Fitzgerald or where older immigrants got jobs cleaning up after them. It was a huge scriptwriting office where people didn't just contemplate laws for the rest of the world but had the means to make the world follow them.

People like writer E.B. White used to say that what makes New York City a vital cosmopolitan centre is that no single idea can dominate its mental skyline for too long. This seems wrong.

If there is a dominant idea in New York, maybe in all of North America, it is that business rules and that economic enterprise is itself a kind of moral activity. It's just that finance and money fly below the radar, pretending not to be there.

Can anybody doubt that inside the WTC decisions were made about who lives and who dies in the world? Wasn't the global currency crisis of 1997 in part caused by New York financial geniuses watching numbers float across computer screens and placing bets on the success and failure of other people's lives by shifting their hedge funds—here, then there—faster than you can click a mouse?

But it has become sacrilege to speak out against high finance, because so many of the people who died in the attack on the WTC did that kind of work. When the TV announced that New York City was up and running, they ran a clip of government officials, police officers and those fabled firemen standing on the balcony overlooking the stock exchange floor ringing that bell to signal that though it had suffered a massive trauma, the market—and by extension the city, the country, and freedom itself—was alive and ready to do business.

And up until that day government was the arch enemy of the market, or so the policymakers and economists told us, especially in America where anti-statism has had a distinguished history. Now these very same people rally around the president and plead for extraordinary state measures for these extraordinary times— in the form of security and discipline, but also bailouts, protectionism, layoffs—while the Left has stepped up to protect individual freedoms and civil liberties.

Violence

Contrary to what some public thinkers have suggested, America does not have a monopoly on state violence. And no matter how you read President Bush's 87-percent approval rating in the year after the attack, Americans are not dupes of some transparent ideology. UBC professor Sunera Thobani was probably right to say that since September 11, dissent has disappeared, but where she and other dissenting voices of the Left go dramatically wrong in explaining how the world should be is that no matter what the politicians and inventive scriptwriters in the media might say, there was nothing new about this war.

Professional pacifists and institutionalized people of higher learning forget that violence has always been both an inexcusable and effective means of changing things. Leave it to the political realists, like the editorial writers at *The Economist*, to spit out the truth of the matter: "The point about being the mightiest nation on earth is that you get to dictate events."

History has never condemned murder itself, only the motive for murder. And like MasterCard, organized murder or war is accepted the world over as a necessity; it is a tool, and the only important question is to which end it is aimed. America sees its military aggression as nothing more than its right to move its body in the direction of a desired goal. It acts like the world's last remaining existentialist, who believes that openness and discussion are empty and trivial, and that action, any action—but especially the fast, hard-hitting kind—is better than political dialogue.

But then amid the sublime realism there are the nauseating platitudes, and the president's elegantly archaic habit of personifying abstractions to play on the most primitive mass instincts.

He saw the world confronting an evil enemy, just as it did in 1945: "Some crimes," he told the United Nations, "are so terrible they offend humanity itself." And he is right. Some crimes do matter more than others. The collapse of the wtc is one of them. The Holocaust is another. We were more pissed off after those events than we ever have been about the genocide of Armenians or East Timorese or Rwandans.

And yet, for all the blunt talk of hitting them with big guns, the massive attack launched on the cave dwellers of Afghanistan was perverse. It amounted to a betrayal of the first principle of civilization: that there is a part of being human that is non-violent and inaccessible to violence—the part that lets us use language and reasoned diplomacy to solve our problems.

From Prepositions to Porno-grammatical Propositions: Bianca and the Need for Restraint

It wasn't the handcuffs that started the problem, but they didn't help, either.

A little more than a decade ago I was in a bar with a colleague gossiping about students and whining about the veneer of compulsory niceness academic culture had put on the university English Department where we were both employed as adjunct professors. After a few drinks he told me, half-jokingly, that he was thinking of taking a job teaching American Lit on a one-year contract at a university in Turkey. "Could you imagine?" he wondered out loud. "There wouldn't be a sexual-harassment officer around for hundreds of miles."

It was wildly inappropriate. Statements like this don't just lead to finger-wagging emails from department heads but, these days, from opprobrious administrators who cite clauses from codes of conduct outlawing verbal microaggressions and other rhetorical widgetries that reconfigure post-secondary teaching with what Laura Kipnis, in her contentious 2015 *Chronicle of Higher Education* essay, "Sexual Paranoia Strikes Academe," calls the melodramatic "fiction" of "helpless victims" and "the fiction of the all-powerful professor." In that piece, which landed Kipnis in a legal mess after a grad student launched a complaint against her, she claimed this: "Sexual paranoia reigns; students are trauma cases waiting to happen. If you wanted to produce a pacified, cowering citizenry, this would be the method."

What my colleague said years ago was, of course, a joke, and I'm pretty sure he wouldn't say it today—not even in jest over too many pints outside earshot—but it was undeniably funny. Or so I thought at the time, and still do. It was also undeniably apropos something that happened. Earlier that Thursday a student had come to see me during office hours and asked a question that was so imprudent, just so wrong on so many levels, that it belonged to one of the more tawdry corners of television—maybe to a minor character's dialogue in a show like *Sons of Anarchy* or to some quasi-pornographic political fiat on *Game of Thrones*.

It had been raining a lot that Thursday and, as people often do when they arrive at a doorway when it's been raining a lot, Bianca—that was the student's name—paused at the door, greeted me with some words explaining her lateness while wiping the water from her coat sleeves and fastening the strap on her umbrella. Something about the bus, the traffic and all this rain, plus her Thursday class started later in the afternoon so she didn't want to be too early. She put the umbrella and her bag on the floor next to the filing cabinet by the door and stepped in, looking around my messy office as people and students often do when they visit. Bookshelves, posters, my bird pictures and Group of Seven prints, whatever happened to be written on the white board. Her eyes stopped where, I know, eyes might stop.

"Handcuffs?" Bianca asked. "And what are *they* for?"

There was nothing wrong with the first part of her question. There was indeed a set of handcuffs dangling from one of the tacks holding up an old *Goodfellas* poster I've been dragging around since grad school. I still have those handcuffs, though they're mostly obscured by decorative pampas grass. My daughter used them as part of a Halloween costume one year, and I brought them to school because I had this notion that they'd help me explain how to use semi-colons—to join two closely related clauses to form a single compound sentence without a coordinating conjunction—and it worked, too, for years. I stopped using them a few years ago after a female colleague told me that an indelicate accoutrement like the handcuffs—no matter how pedagogically effective—might be construed these days as more than bad optics. *"They're threatening,"* I remember her telling me in the mock overbearing tone of a campus bureaucrat, with her finger wagging at me.

Bianca's second question, though, was a finely measured clause bookended by an innocuous conjunction and a slightly less than innocent preposition, but it was spliced with a pronoun that was so frictional that I can only *italicize* it to suggest the tone with which she delivered it. And that was the problem. Ludwig Wittgenstein, who believed that the source of most misunderstandings between people was linguistic, said in his *Philosophical Investigations* that "in most cases, the meaning of a word is its use," and what Bianca meant by that pronoun had less to do with its dictionary meaning than with how she used it.

"And what are *they* for?"

It wasn't even a question. Not really, but then it wasn't a statement, either. Function words like pronouns and articles and conjunctions, like the social psychologist James Pennebaker says in *The Secret Life of Pronouns*, can reveal more about someone's personality than nouns and verbs, and Bianca's pronoun, which was cleaved in that clause like a golden strand suspended from a honey dripper, was slurred, what a phonologist would call "re-laxed pronunciation." It wasn't directly coquettish but it wasn't free of innuendo either; it was the kind of interrogative that, in a suitable context—a BDSM bar, for example, or when your part-ner role-plays the saucy wench to boost your vanilla sex life—might be understood as an incitement to discourse, an invitation to the kind of dialogue that would tremble on the brink of inde-cency. But in the respectable context of a teaching institution, it could spell trouble.

Grammatically compromised but rhetorically stimulated—and, I still believe, intentionally stimulating—that clause was like an evocative mise en scène from a favourite movie—like when Sharon Stone crosses her legs in *Basic Instinct* or, better still, when Joaquin Phoenix tells his Siri-like phone-sex partner Samantha in *Her* that he'd touch her neck and we hear Scarlett Johansson's virtually orgasmic moan. I've spent some time fleshing out the linguistic context and the empirical backstory of this scene, and, yes, I'm sure I've fictionalized it at the edges, maybe even coloured it with the retroactive wish-fulfillment thrust of my own middle-aged imagination, but the basic facts remain true in the constellation of that wet Thursday afternoon in November. The old-school structuralist Roland Barthes once said that "the first thing we love is a scene." "A curtain opens," he writes, "and what had not yet ever been seen is devoured by the eyes": "The scene consecrates the object," he says, and in that particular scene—the weather, the light cast on that Thursday in Novem-ber, the stuff besides the handcuffs Bianca saw but didn't ask me about, the question she posed in just that manner—consecrated something I'd never experienced before, and probably couldn't experience any more.

Like every good scene, whether in a film, novel or an ongoing professional conversation, this one had antecedents. I wouldn't say it was foreshadowed, but it wasn't entirely unexpected. Bianca was supposed to come see me at 10:30 that morning because she'd nearly failed her poetry essay the week before. She was a classic C-student—"backbone of the nation," as Vladimir Nabokov called them—whose swaggering sense of her own intellectual abilities and ravenous narcissism never could grasp that her written work just wasn't that good. Or maybe she didn't care.

During the first class of the term, when I was doing my usual schtick about needing to learn some poetry—not to get them in touch with their inner expressive emo-genius but to straighten the lines of their thinking—she raised her hand and announced, in the first of many non sequiturs, that poetry is useless except on greeting cards and with music, then said something about people who write poetry just *need to get laid more* or something along those lines. Bianca often blurted out things that I could only manage to relate back to what we happened to be talking about with some rhetorical contortions of my own, but in the small universe of that group of thirty-five students, she had a pass because she was slightly older than most of them and because, to put it indelicately, she looked like she'd walked out of a Russ Meyer film set. They were prominent, nearly audible and always, well, just sort of *there*, occupying space like an overload student you let into your class even though it's already crowded, and though it's impolite and probably sexist to say so, if you could have seen *how* she walked into class and took her seat in the mosh pit—the front row between the lectern and desk, where the most talkative but not always the brightest ones usually sit—I'm sure you would say that she knew how to invoke them. And who could blame her? Joan Jett once said, "Girls have balls, they're just a little higher up, that's all," and Bianca definitely had balls.

The real backstory, though, was that she had jammed up my teaching just over a week before she came to my office that Thursday, at the end of the class just before their first big essay, the one she failed. They were going to write an analysis on an e.e. cummings poem. It was the last ten minutes of class, and we were about to do a quick review in which they'd ask things and I'd write answers down, but I ended up writing "Anal. on ee cum" at the top of the board. A few of them snickered, Bianca loudest, and within a second my arm swooped back to add a second set of "m" humps to my unintentionally crude abbreviation for cummings—I would have liked to tack on an "ysis" to the "Anal" part but couldn't squeeze it in there—but Bianca and a few others, doing what stronger students do when they sense a weakness in their teacher, snickered even louder to signify, I imagine, a victory in my apparent embarrassment. You learn to not get easily embarrassed in front of an audience of young people, and I wasn't really, but then about an hour after class I got an email from Bianca saying she couldn't make my office hour but that she had a question about the forthcoming essay. The subject line read *"the anal/cum business"*—very funny—and in it she said this:

The poem didn't make any sense 2 me til u said 'the voice of ur eyes' is a mixed metaphor, because I think this is about a woman who wants to get with the guy but because she's a cliché who doesn't make it about sex but about feelings or am I wrong? If I said this in my essay would it be the anal on cum(!) u want?

Notwithstanding the savagery of her misreading of "somewhere I have never travelled," which was worse even than the wanton butchery of her grammar and disregard for logic, I responded with more brevity than austerity and said she should get in the habit of disciplining her sentences, even in emails, if she wanted to improve in her writing, but that was a formality because after a few classes I had already figured that much of what she said, whether haphazardly in class or in an email, would squirm with the kind of suggestiveness that comes from disordered words that, I also figured, she must have considered a perfectly natural form of communication. That may be unfair, but I guess I pigeonhole students the way they do me. Bianca's primary interest in sex, clothing and prosperity, I imagined, left little time for any sustained concern with the formalities of syntax, grammar and punctuation. Not that her email was sexual, though it did seem to be at the time hieroglyphically obscene in a humorous sort of way. I'm sure I probably wondered if there was some administrative memo I should have read but just shoved into my desk, something about how to deal with female students who might be too, you know, forward. At the time I'd heard lots about male students harassing female colleagues and, of course, even more about male profs and female students—think *Oleanna*, *The Life of David Gale*, *The Squid and the Whale*—and though I'm certain that's how the trope usually happens, I'd never heard of anything quite like this. Nor, for that matter, would I have been inclined to think about it much beyond the blithe wondering I gave it. Not at the time, I mean.

But all that's changed, as has the nature of post-secondary schooling, for both good and bad, largely because it seems inseparable from all the talk of "trigger warnings" and "safe spaces," "rape culture" and the student-as-consumer model that most post-secondary schools now adopt. On the one hand, at least the matter has been put into public discussion. In the spring of 2016 the McGill University newspaper put out a piece that opened with the claim that "sexual harassment of students by professors is slowly becoming a central and very public issue." Citing well-known recent cases at UBC and UQAM, Geneviève Mercier-Dalphond wrote that "professors have been known to take advantage of their position of authority to 'treat their classrooms like real-life Tinder accounts,'" which is no doubt as true as the trope of the student-teacher affair is a convention in popular culture. That line she quoted about Tinder came from an article that appeared a year earlier called "Let's Talk about Teacher," in which the anony-mous writer tells an admirably honest account of getting into and having a relationship with one of her profs whom, ultimately, she learned had a reputation for hitting on his female students. "I was devastated for a long time after I realized that I wasn't anything but a mildly entertaining wet hole to this man. I felt betrayed," she wrote. "I had been dedicated to his ideas and to his work. ... But I guess my respect didn't really mean shit to him, on any level." Then there are those in the defensive camp who, because they deign to defend what seems indefensible, sound insensitive by comparison. Like Katie Roiphe, for example, who in a 2013 *Slate* piece wrote a defence of an American philosophy prof who "lost everything" because a twenty-six-year-old student accused him of sexual harassment, much to the delight of the media, who seem to love this sort of narrative. "It is true," Roiphe said, "that a female student has the unspoken power to whisper two words and ruin an entire career," which I think is "true" even though I'd only write that with scare-quotes around it. That same year, the always notorious Camille Paglia wrote a *Time* essay on the appar-ently "wildly overblown claims" about all the sexual assaults happening on American campuses, a topic so overdetermined that I can't think of a single guy who would—or could—say that. "Too many young middle-class women," she wrote with that trademark common-sense polemic that always sounds partly right, even if it sounds like right-wing victim-blaming, "seem to expect adult life to be an extension of their comfortable, overprotected homes. But the world remains a wilderness. The price of women's modern freedoms is personal responsibility for vigilance and self-defense." More recently, the less impetuous Laura Kipnis, in last year's *Chronicle* piece, lamented the rise of sexual paranoia on campuses. "When I was in college," she said in one of the many lines that pushed some student activists to launch a legal case that resulted in a seventy-two-day investigation, "hooking up with professors was more or less part of the curriculum. ... It's not that I didn't make my share of mistakes, or act stupidly and inchoately, but it was embarrassing, not traumatizing."

Nobody would deny that there are some profs who do treat their classes like Tinder, and most of them are guys, I'm sure. But there are cases, too, of course, in which students might actually want to sleep with their teachers, and maybe when that wish is psychologically sound, the desire isn't for physical attraction but is just a thing to do, a life experience. A woman I know once berated me for "preying" on a female grad student after I told her about a temptation that had opened itself up to me on one occasion, then years later told me without flinching that when she was in college she dated and had "relations" with her former high school English teacher who fancied her because she was "curious." I can understand why she would have been curious, though I had a hard time understanding why it was that when I admitted to a similar temptation I was "preying."

Was Bianca's attempt at nurturing a private language with me more than a decade ago a form of harassment? Not unless we incriminate phatic pronouns. Did that dumb abbreviation I wrote on the board enable it? Maybe, but what about it? Was her butchered grammar intended to mock my mistake or was it, together with that enclosed exclamation mark in her email, supposed to generate a bawdy dimension to our communication? Were my intentions anything but pedagogically Platonic? Probably. For all my paranoid wonderings since that time, awkward emails like hers certainly give the cerebral cadence of teaching poetry a thrumming jolt, even if that jolt comes at the expense of good grammar and decency. Bianca was, as far as I could tell, what Angela Carter calls a "Sadean woman," a woman who isn't as much the object of desire (as in the garden-variety romance novel) but is, as the Marquis de Sade knew, a body of desires that are just as immediate, just as forward and licentious, and no less indecent than a man's.

I imagine most people who teach have encountered students with whom they have awkward, sexually strained or just baffling language relations, more likely early in their careers. There have been a few students in my classes who've made the kind of appeals that Aristotle never really talked about in his books on persuasion. Sometimes it's rhetorically in the form of that simple but pornographically mythical question, "Is there anything I can do to improve my mark?" And sometimes it's more physical, which might be, I'll admit, titillating but not more than it is scary because it violates professional imperatives by pushing referential communication aside and introducing more metalingual language games, or flirting.

Years ago, around the same time I had Bianca, a student from my CanLit class came to my office to ask about the novel she wanted to write on for her final paper. *Cabbagetown*, Hugh Garner's classic story about a white working-class kid in Depression-era Toronto, is simple. She sat there in the chair not asking any questions but repeating the plot, which is what students often do when they need reassurance that the story they read is actually the same one you read, but when she recounted the scene in which Ken meets the farmer's wife in the kitchen, she leaned forward, as if she was going to finally pose a relevant question related to her paper, and asked if the farmer's wife actually opened her shirt and offered her breasts to Ken, which in fact she does. In a wacky twist of literal performativity, as she asked, she unfastened two or three buttons on her blouse and pulled the placket aside—consciously or unconsciously, I have no idea—perhaps in the same way the wife does, though I don't know because Garner's narrative cuts out and goes elsewhere. Years later at another school I had a student who wanted to write her research paper on the rhetorical branding of Sexaholics Anonymous because, as I came to learn through too many meetings with her about this odd case study during my office hours, she was a sexaholic, or so she claimed. Like Bianca, she was older, a high-octane business student who would always schedule appointments even though I told her and everybody else that they could just come by during my scheduled hours. After one meeting she stood up and stepped towards the door but hesitated, briefly, or just long enough to reach around to her lower back, lift her shirt and place a finger between her bare skin and the top part of her thong undergarment, crook her finger, pull up and say, "See?" I could see it, of course, because I was looking as she exited, that finger unwinding itself as she stepped into the hall. It was bizarre, mostly because we hadn't talked about this "sexaholism" she allegedly lived and wanted to write about, but for the next few years it was hard not to think "thong" whenever I'd see her around campus. It was more fascinating than disturbing, though my institution, following the administer-*everything* policy of most schools, now has what they call the BIT, a Behavioural Intervention Team that deals with "students whose behaviours are concerning, disruptive, or threatening." It's absolutely necessary, mind you, which was made clear to me one evening around midnight when I got a call from some sergeant at the Vancouver Police who told me that one of my students, a mature student who seemed quite normal if somewhat clingy, came to headquarters and asked to be taken into psychiatric care and named me as her personal contact.

I imagine the violation of professional conduct or, to use the proprietorial metaphor currently in vogue, "boundaries" is always part of the appeal in cases in which teachers and students engage in romantic or sexual liaisons. Doing things that are wrong, as anybody who's stolen hotel amenities or cheated on their taxes knows, can be enticing. De Sade believed that the one condition of sensual pleasure is crime, which I'm sure might be true in a theoretical sense, and Georges Bataille, a writer obsessed with excesses of all kinds, said in his essay on de Sade that "erotic activity always takes place at the expense of the forces committed to their combat."

When I got my first good teaching job, I went with a few new hires to a "mixer" where we met a group of grad students who told us about this "Boff a prof" thing, which none of us had ever heard of before. That's why the three grad students were there, or so they intimated, and that's why they sat down to drinks with us lowly adjunct faculty members. This unofficial contest, for which there were no prizes except the more or less private notoriety and probable embarrassment that comes with a romp with an older guy, sounded like it may have been a "thing" in the 1970s, though I have heard the expression only one time since.

I did answer Bianca's slippery question about the handcuffs. I said something like, "Just decoration, that's all." There was more push and pull that was all too harmless. She brought the essay with her, and though I can't recall a single thing she wrote in that mess on cummings, I'm sure I just repeated what I always write in the margins: *Spelling, Subject-Verb Agreement, Comma splice. Pronoun? What does this "it" mean? Dangling modifier. Proof? What kind of hallucination is this?* The voluptuous imperfection of her written words warranted these queries and much more. On some days I believe with the fervour of a recently acquired faith that I can discipline a student's language well enough for communication to happen. I believe, just as one might believe in the assistance of angels or the regulating comfort of a Buddhist mantra, that grammar is the only method of straightening the lines of a student's thinking. When I told her that an average of two mistakes per sentence is unacceptable at this level of study, she called me something I've never been called before and said something that I've never heard since. "Alright, Captain English," she said and then went into the all too typical complaint that bad grammar didn't matter to the "ideas" she was trying to put across, and that for sure grammar mistakes couldn't be enough to give a paper a C-, which is what I gave her, though I should have failed her and told her as much. Then, in an admirable and even logical compound sentence, she connected what I said about her need to discipline her writing to her own apparent need to be handcuffed. Because she said it in a way that suggested she was just putting that out there, which is the way with these sorts of propositions, I pretended not to hear and plowed through with more about split infinitives and syntax. It wasn't for another decade, when a female colleague admitted in the context of her defence of *Fifty Shades of Grey* that she felt the allure of bondage and had fantasized about being tied, that I heard something quite as innovative as Bianca's porno-grammar. Nevertheless, I did think about that compound sentence, probably too much, but I believe I thought about it academically. I remember from teaching the work of that elaborate eighteenth-century sexual fantasist, the Marquis de Sade, that there is a striking theoretical similarity between what happens in sexual situations and the ministrations of pain and discipline, though I had never thought of the kinky kind of discipline in terms of grammar, but there may be that connection. And there is, as I read in Barthes years later when I was trying to understand that connection, something called a "porno-grammar," an inventory of patterns and structures that can be applied to sex as much as to language.

Though the job of teaching is increasingly administered and the students are increasingly treated more like children—twenty-five is the new eighteen, or is it thirty?—unlike a lot of other professions, teaching has always required a degree of intimacy that can, when minds and situations collude, lead to unintended dangers, even if those dangers remain more rhetorical than real. That intimacy goes back to the story of Héloïse and Abelard, the medieval French student and teacher who engaged in a tryst that still resonates across our culture, from Rousseau to Mark Twain, Cole Porter to Frank Black, *The Sopranos* to *Eternal Sunshine of the Spotless Mind*. "Eroticism, covert or declared, fantasised or enacted, is inwoven in teaching, in the phenomenology of mastery and discipleship," the cosmopolitan literary critic George Steiner once said. You couldn't get away with saying that sort of thing in a departmental meeting these days, and I wouldn't want to try, though I suspect that secretly a lot of people believe that it's true. "This elemental fact has been trivialised," Steiner continues—and I'd definitely not say this next part out loud any more—"by a fixation on sexual harassment."

The job is safer now, less open to risqué rhetorical flourishes and certainly to the sort of contentious and controversial language games and body theatrics that Bianca brought into my office that Thursday, but the students are, on the whole, far less captivating, and I don't mean entertaining. It may be because I am older, but I think they are much more like children than they used to be even as little as ten years ago and, like children, they are indeed more vulnerable and innocent and so in need of protection, less experienced in pretty much everything. It's safer, both for me and, thankfully, for them, too, but for all that, I miss students like Bianca, notwithstanding the constant danger and disorder she brought with her whenever she appeared at my door.

Bianca and the Blackbirds: How Vladimir Nabokov Saved Me from Referential Mania

There's a scene in Vladimir Nabokov's *Laughter in the Dark* in which Axel, the rakish middle-aged artist, turns to his way-too-young lover, Margot, and delivers an impeccable aphorism. "A certain man once lost a diamond cuff-link in the wide blue sea, and twenty years later, on the exact day, a Friday apparently, he was eating a large fish—but there was no diamond inside. That's what I like about coincidence." These little word-jewels are what I like about Nabokov. Life is capricious and open to chance, not held together by some cosmic duct tape that harmonizes random events in a state of metaphysical awesomeness. And yet, even though reason and Nabokov tell us that coincidences don't just happen, we know that it's only in detecting and recognizing flukes and fortuities that the deliberate familiarity of an ordinary life can be refashioned as extraordinary, enchanting and at times even thrilling.

My job—teaching English Literature to college students—isn't that exhilarating. Like being the night watchman at a museum or a volunteer shelver at a public library, it's rewarding in an intangible way and it's always more pedestrian than provocative. When something memorable happens, it's to fictional characters on paper or screen; I'm supposed to remain abstract and nonplussed by scandalous shenanigans. But there was this one time, one afternoon years ago, when something happened in my office that was so unnervingly wanton and such a bamboozling conundrum that it left me metaphysically overwhelmed.

"Bianca" was a student in my English class. Older, around twenty-five or so, and Southeastern European by birth, she struck me as well versed in the ways of the world, certainly compared to the more morally chaste younger students, though academically she was extraordinarily average. A classic femme fatale who adapted to the brazen aesthetic of sex-positive feminism, Bianca announced her presence the first day of class almost a decade ago by declaring that feminists "need a good fuck." Always one for theatrics, she's what you get when you slip a coquette like Lauren Bacall or Lana Turner into the cast of Lena Dunham's *Girls*. She was, in short, a woman with a gifted cleavage and a mediocre mind who knew she could often use the first in the service of the second.

I hadn't heard from Bianca for a few years when she emailed and asked if I remembered her and could she come by my office? She was writing a paper for a grad seminar on postmodern language games and wanted to talk literary shop. I obliged with a time—2:30 on a Tuesday—and mentioned that I happened to be teaching Nabokov's short story "Symbols and Signs" that very week and goading my first-year students, in the same course she'd taken with me a few years before, in slow textual analyses of the narrative.

She was on time, but I was with another student. This one was crying, like the sensitive ones sometimes do when they realize that their work isn't the A-level work the high school teachers said it was. I don't remember most of the criers but I remember this one—Harry Potter glasses and an unironic Hello

Kitty knapsack—because during the fifteen minutes she was in my office I had four or five phone calls. The first was a guy who wanted to speak to Charlie-somebody, and the rest were all hang ups. It was irritating, but all that ringing alleviated the task of trying to make my criticism of the girl's banal analysis of a sentence in "Symbols and Signs" sound more like a consolation to her wounded self-esteem. In any case, persistent phone calls can make you go fucking ape shit with paranoia, and even Nabokov knew this because at the end of that story someone calls for a "Charlie" two times, and the third is a hang up.

This was when I first considered that this parcel of time on a dreary Tuesday afternoon in November just might be, contrary to the routines that structured typical afternoons, textured with a metaphysical thread of tattered references and allusions that were just a little too strange, though at the time I didn't think the phone calls could have possibly foreshadowed that something wildly inappropriate was about to happen. And I still can't. But then coincidence is a seductive spark ignited by memory, and what's so fascinating about memory, as Nabokov writes in his autobiography, "is the masterly use it makes of innate harmonies when gathering to its fold the suspended and wandering tonalities of the past." It was months, probably closer to a year and maybe even longer, before I remembered in my own "suspended and wandering tonalities" that Bianca, who was pacing outside my office while I was with the crier, had a phone in her hand. Which isn't strange in itself, not really. Maybe she wanted to tumble my dominoes of fortuity. Even Aristotle points out in *The Poetics* that coincidences are "most striking when they have an air of design," and if she did disguise her voice and place those calls, then it was a striking design.

The crier exited, and Bianca entered. She didn't mention the ringing, but sitting down in the chair the crier had just vacated, she leaned forward. Wasn't it bizarre, she asked in a mock conspiratorial voice, that one of the important signs or symbols in Nabokov's story is a crying girl and that a real one was just sitting in this chair? I agreed, it was, and so were the phone calls. Life imitated art in the weather pattern, too, and then again in our ensuing conversation when I learned that it was Bianca's birthday the next day. I pointed out that it's also a raining birthday in "Symbols and Signs."

If there were a fate story that overlapped with my life I wouldn't want it to be this one. It's a dreary narrative about an elderly Russian couple who go visit their deranged son at an asylum for his birthday but are turned away because he has tried to commit suicide again. I like it because it's short and because Nabokov—a literary genius but a pretentious dick—puts you on a wild-goose chase looking for "signs" or "symbols" in the story that are supposed to make reading the story hook up with the son's delusional condition. Believing that "everything happening around him is a veiled reference to his personality and existence," he considers every detail in his environment—the clouds, mannequins, his exhalations—as somehow being about him.

The thing is, when you read the story, you fall into the same system of paranoid delusions because each detail in the narrative is designed to charm you into your own "referential mania": even if you want to read right past them, you can't. On the contrary, like the compulsive paranoiac in the story, you find something relevant in each reference and suture them all to a bigger pattern of meaning. The postmodern joke is that the parents experience things—the rain, a girl crying, a late bus, the phone, a fledgling blackbird and so on—that are so obviously random and unrelated to their son's fate, but we can't help but think they're all references that tell us, conclusively, what the story is *really* about. Even though it's really only about an old couple in New York City who want to visit their fucked-up son on his birthday but end up going home—where someone calls asking for Charlie. You can't help overreading it and making it into something it's not. It's like Thomas Pynchon says, "There is something comforting—religious, if you want—about paranoia," partly because we can't stand when "nothing is connected to anything." Whatever the case, Nabokov's story is a great introduction to the "arbitrary" relationship between a signifier and signified—a word and its idea—which is a core part of literary theory-speak but which is pretty useful in understanding why any semiotically charged cultural practice—from horoscopes to modernist poetry, from road signs to online dating profiles—are so evocative to us even if we know they're arbitrary.

Though Bianca and I did talk about Ferdinand de Saussure, the Swiss linguist who came up with this concept of arbitrariness, we didn't dwell on the kinks in the envelope of analogical weirdness that meshed this parcel of real-time things—a ringing phone, the crier, the weather and birthday—with their anchors in the Nabokov story. Instead, she told me about life in Toronto, that she'd been there a year, loved postmodernism and wanted to teach Comp Lit one day, and—finally—that she needed help with her essay on the erotics of language in *Lolita* and *Laughter in the Dark*. She was working with a "theory" of reading she got from *The Pleasure of the Text,* a book by Roland Barthes, a French literary celebrity who was killed by a laundry truck back when students were all down with the zany language of postmodernism.

This business about the "erotics of language" in Bianca's essay, coupled with the title of that one Nabokov novel—both novels, actually, though the second, an earlier attempt at the same kind of story, doesn't have the twisted reputation—probably suggests that my trivial narrative about the collusion of fiction with reality is going to a perverted end. Though Bianca had graduated years before that November visit, it's pretty much always scary—and destabilizing in an existential way that dislodges you from the walls of your ethical self—when a female student is in your office talking about particular books and particular themes. Bianca's Frenchman wrote, "The pleasure of the text is that moment when my body pursues its own ideas—for my body does not have the same ideas as I do," and anybody who's had a bodily reaction when reading bad porn knows he's right. But people who read and talk about what they're reading can't go around living by this truth. It's bad optics. Maybe it's true that nothing says risqué like a discussion of metaphor and syntax in suggestive novels that most normal people won't ever read, but the overdetermined setting of an academic office triggers, in the compulsory pornography of our time, a series of tawdry conclusions, which is its own kind of referential mania. And which is why my door is always open, especially when I'm with a female student and doubly especially when she's a morally emancipated one who wants to talk about mature subject matter like a fleshy e.e. cummings poem or an Angela Carter story. Or Nabokov, though this guy's sentences are so compounded and his allusions so convoluted that indecencies remain hidden to most people or only alluded to through tedious indirection that most won't bother to follow.

My door was open the day Bianca came to visit, and it stayed that way until something happened that was stranger still than the trifling conspiracy of fiction with reality I was just going on about. I was rambling on about Nabokov's sentences. I think it was how his suspended sentences say indirectly what his characters are doing when we think they might be fucking but don't know for sure because his language is so murky. She said she was writing about the "erotics" of his writing and wanted to argue that the intermittent suggestiveness in his sentences, the fact that he goes on and on and teases readers with quick flits and flashes of sexuality, is like a striptease. It was more eyebrow angle, and it was around here that Bianca reached across my desk with her left hand to the jar of jelly beans I keep beside the phone. Maybe it was her fingers or maybe the arm of her black raincoat, but on the way there she dislodged the handset from the phone and it dropped between the desk and her chair.

She must have gotten up, and I probably did, too, or half-stood and leaned, nudged her chair back and pulled up the handset up by its cord, because when I looked up again I saw that Bianca was at the door, which was now more closed than it was when she came in. And apparently in those four or five steps it took her to get from the chair to the door she significantly altered the structure of her apparel because what I saw was a vertical column of bare skin framed by a partially opened black raincoat—unbuttoned or unzipped, I don't know which—and punctuated only twice with minimalist underthings. She leaned back into the jackets and sweaters I keep hanging on the back of the door and it clicked shut. If any of this happened in a novel or a film I'd say it was an important dialectical image or core *mise en scène* and talk theoretically about composition and proxemics and psychological setting, but here, at 2:30 in the afternoon in my second-floor college office, I had no idea what to say.

There's nothing quite so wanton or wantonly incoherent in Nabokov. I know what Bianca was disclosing with that subtle re-organization of her clothing, but in-the-flesh embodiments of literary principles like the "erotics of language" aren't supposed to happen to me. I was, and still am, looking for references, for something I may have missed in "Symbols and Signs" or in those novels Bianca wanted to talk to me about, that explains or legit-imates the malapropism of a partially clothed woman leaning back against the inside of my office door. Margot in *Laughter in the Dark* was a conniving temptress, and Lolita, well, I'm never sure what to say about her.

I stood there, uncomfortably, in the Tuesday afternoon low-key light of my office while this woman who said she wanted to talk about words leaned against my door in a scandalous but entirely fetching state of dishabille, and signified herself silently. I wasn't even sure if I was the intended referent or part of the sign or even if the scene was her attempt at illustrating the arbitrary relation-ship between a signifier and signified for some secret grad-school project. So I just stood there staring at that vertical strip of white barely punctuated with two horizontal references of clothing and spellbound by the uncanny pornography of it all. Barthes, Bianca's French theorist who went on about the "pleasures of the text," once asked, "Is not the most erotic portion of a body where the garment gapes?" Theoretically speaking, the answer has to be yes. I know Freud was right to say that repression of sexual instinct is needed in a civilized society for it to work, but let's face it, when a woman strikes this semiotic pose in your office, you can't help but wonder if Herbert Marcuse, the guy who reread Freud from a per-missive point of view and said that eros is the truly constructive impulse of civilization, might have been even more right.

This event became more coherent to me when, improbably, Nabokov's story pushed itself back into the narrative. Bianca stood there, armed in that long raincoat and waiting for me to say or, maybe, to do something, but fortuitously—or maybe not?—two more quirks intervened to nudge this suspended moment away from sheer caprice back to the world of incomprehensibly meaningful signs and symbols. The phone, still in my hand, started making that irritating sound a phone makes when it's off the hook too long, and this, I think, effectively compromised the intended tone of the scene. And then, as if on cue, just as we both became aware of that sound, a bird flew to my window. I heard but didn't notice until Bianca, with a look that signified comical vexation, said, "A bird. Unfuckingreal. The phone. And I have red toes." She was looking behind me, and when I turned to look I saw the black wings scrum along the window and fly off.

I didn't ask about the red toes. There's a reference to red toes and a bird in "Symbols and Signs," and red is obviously a sign—or symbol?—of passion and sexuality. But the sheer congestion of fictional coincidences in the temporal continuum that afternoon weirded me out way more than its impropriety. The "girl with dark hair...was weeping," "the telephone rang again," "a tiny unfledged bird was helplessly twitching." The details nudged their way from Nabokov's story into my office, some by design but mostly as a function of a remarkable shift in the narrative of an afternoon that was punctuated with an enticing personification of the "erotics of language" that, unclothed, leaned back against my door until it shut.

And there are more stories about the memorable Bianca. She flirted obsessively, shifting attention from comma splices and mishandling of semicolons with compulsive leg crossings and inordinately low leans across the desk, sustained stares, and the time she asked a borderline unsavoury question about the pair of costume handcuffs I have hanging on my wall. A couple of years after she leaned back against my door in that unclothed state, she sent me a copy of the paper she wrote on Nabokov's stories. It was decent, but all I really remember of it is the epigram, which came from her French theorist: "Is not the most erotic portion of a body where the garment gapes?"

In the subdued rush of references—her visit to my office during my Nabokov week, the phone calls, Charlie, the rain, the crying girl, the bird, the birthday—I convinced myself that this sliver of time on a Tuesday afternoon in November was so patterned, so symbolically charged with significant details. I think the impulse to find a pattern in one's life, to find causes and reasons for the events we experience that push thinking away from the banal towards the metaphysical, and maybe even to the spiritual—yes, even in tawdry narratives involving lascivious characters named "Bianca"—is greater than our seemingly absolute knowledge that no such patterns can possibly exist. Nabokov says in his novel *Ada* that "some law of logic should fix the number of coincidences, in a given domain, after which they cease to be coincidences, and form, instead, the living organism of a new truth." I have no idea what kind of "new truth" the coincidences on that Tuesday afternoon pointed towards. It wasn't fate that connected her to me as much as it was a voluptuous appetite for Nabokov and literary theory, though it was a thrill I'm bound—referential maniac that I am—to vaunt to the level of enchanting, beautiful things.

Purloined Gigabytes and the Secret Capable of Taking Place between Us

> Secrets, silent, stony sit in the dark palaces of both our hearts: secrets weary of their tyranny: tyrants willing to be dethroned.
>
> —James Joyce, Ulysses

Last summer a group called "Impact Team" hacked into the extramarital-affair website Ashley Madison and threatened to go public with information about its members unless the parent company, Toronto-based Avid Life Media, shut down the popular social network platform for cheaters. ALM called the hacker's bluff and lost. A month later, on August 18, in a move aimed at shaming the clients who embraced their "Life's Short. Have an Affair" brand, they released more than thirty gigabytes of data, including the names, emails and sexual tastes of people who were dumb enough to register with their real names. About 32 million of them, although Gizmodo reported that only about 12,000 belonged to real women—the rest were fembot "engagers" designed to lure men into AM with the promise of clicking their way to a secret playground of ravenously sexed married women who just weren't getting enough at home. In their press release the hackers called out "the fraud, deceit, and stupidity of ALM and their members" and followed up with "Too bad for ALM, you promised secrecy but didn't deliver."

It was all very dramatic for a few days, and some people were discreetly freaked out: the women and men who, having thought that fucking people other than their spouses would deliver them from banality to bliss, could deceive, and the spouses who, having mistook their relationships as havens of idyllic togetherness, could be so deceived. But then "tales of ecstasy," as the adulterous narrator in Josephine Hart's soul-shredding novel *Damage* says, "are endless tales of failure." And just as they have since Zeus hooked up with women other than Hera, and Hagar had that tryst with Abraham, stories where carnal pleasure fuses with moral agony provided the media—the *Wall Street Journal* and *Chronicle of Higher Education* no less than *Cosmopolitan* and *TMZ*—with a predictable cast of finger-wagging saints and scandalized sinners, their betrayals and disgraces exposed, their excuses and rationalizations, the marital strife and divorces, a cottage industry of post-adultery lawyers and psychologists offering services online, and tragically even a couple of suicides. A few months after the hack the antivirus genius John McAfee went public and said the problem was that AM "offered services predicated on the imagery of sex and trust at the same time," and of course everybody knows that sex and trust aren't good bedfellows. "What made Ashley Madison so significant," he said, in a striking metaphysical flourish, "was the loss of innocence and potential future awareness that it caused."

I was sitting with my mother in the waiting room of a cancer clinic in Hamilton when I saw a CNN report on the story that Tuesday last August. You'd think a big whiff of mortality would curb interest in a silly tabloid story about people who cheat, but as the reporter was explaining how viewers could find out if people they knew were among the scoundrels who were outed, everybody in the room seemed captivated, including my mother, who said she really didn't understand what all the fuss was about. Some websites appeared on-screen, and I noticed a woman sitting across from me reach for hers, so I grabbed my phone, too, found one of them and started putting in email addresses. It was a Pandora's Box of perverse schadenfreude tinged with something strangely Freudian, sitting there wondering each time I hit "return" what the moral verdict would be. My spouse's email addresses, my ex, friends, coworkers, family, even my own. Shocked isn't the right word, but I was surprised. Not just because some of them returned "Oh no! pwned!"—would I ever see these people without an invisible scarlet letter hovering above their heads?—but because my address came back clean. No, it's not what you think—not exactly. It's not a secret. It was for some months a decade ago, but I still hesitate to talk about it today, directly, because although a secret only exists because we have language to keep it, when it's told the secrecy ends. And then some secrets, like this one, are strangely the ones we're really not ashamed to have done in the first place.

Things—leaves, your body, a marriage—tend to fall apart, get worn down and frayed by the natural tendency to impermanence. Al Purdy once wrote in a lovely poem that "everything fades / and wavers into something else," which are lines I often dragged into my head years ago when I first considered reanimating my years with the sensuality that had drained from them. If it's not death and impermanence, then it's sex that is literature's foremost preoccupation, and adultery is one of its foundational motifs because it opens that perpetual conflict between body and mind. Infidelity always looks so damn good and right when we read about it in a book or watch it on-screen, doesn't it? "Those who restrain their desire," William Blake says in *The Marriage of Heaven and Hell*, "do so because theirs is weak enough to be restrained," a lovely sentiment that can, with small effort, vindicate the most scandalous bedhopping shenanigans we see on *Mad Men* or *The Good Wife*. "If adultery is wickedness then so is food," says Kurt Vonnegut in *Hocus Pocus*. "Both make me feel so much better afterward." And one of the most memorable lines in the award-winning animation from 2015, Charlie Kaufman's *Anomalisa*, comes from the married motivational guru, Michael, who's in an apathetic funk until he meets and beds the anomalous Lisa: "Our time is limited, we forget that," he says, in an aphorism that to me sounds like it's pulled from the same rhetorical bag of wisdom as AM's slogan.

Literary insights like these refashion philandering as a desire to make life—especially during those crisis-prone middle years when you realize you're going to end—into a work of art, complete with a plot that has climaxes and features round characters who periodically stray outside the bounds of social propriety by relinquishing control of their primal instincts and following the pulsating narrative thrum of their mortal carnality to the most voluptuous, immoral of places. Maybe that pulsation is just the result of a very basic anxiety we all have, what Julian Barnes in *The Sense of an Ending* calls "another of our fears: that Life wouldn't turn out to be like Literature." And isn't the fear of living an unliterary life, even more than the fear of death to which it must be related—just like Freud said, "eros," our life instinct, is related to our "death instinct"—a palpable, legitimate and a good fear for us to have?

It was for me. So like a lot of literary characters who latch onto the real or imagined banality of their own lives to justify the musk-scented rush of bodies colliding in illicit pools of sexual abandon—Austen's Henry Crawford, Flaubert's Emma Bovary, Updike's Rabbit Angstrom, Megan in Hawkins's *The Girl on the Train*—and like a lot more real people, somewhere during the narrative of my midlife I decided that the little thrills, like smoking a joint after tucking your kid in or flirting with your wife's friend in the kitchen at that Christmas party, just wouldn't do it. Only a voluptuous yearning, I thought in a moment of unintentional clarity, the kind that leads to the sublime disorientation of landing in a stranger's bed, could give life the semblance of art, make it feel literary in characterization and plot. I still wonder if that's just an absurdly pretentious way of saying I wanted to get laid. There's nothing more ordinary than an ordinary guy's flight from bourgeois ordinariness, right? I know. As common as beards and selfies among millennials, infidelity is, like Nabokov once said, "a most conventional way to rise above the conventional."

It just didn't seem all that conventional at the time, and it was a lot easier than I expected. Notwithstanding those stories about fembots bamboozling millions of guys on AM—*Fortune* called it "a male-dominated platform nearly devoid of women"—I was struck by the number of all-too-real women who were not only ready to engage in the compulsory discursive foreplay but willing to execute face-to-face meetings. I was probably older, and I'm sure I didn't measure up to the romance novel preferences—in height, looks, endowment, musculature—I sussed out in some profiles, but it didn't take long for fumbling messages to evolve, in a few cases, into a mutual degree of curiosity about the person on the other end of the screen that lead to those passionately awkward first meetings where both parties negotiating a prospective adultery could see what, if anything, might happen, and when.

It's true that sex-fuelled social media platforms like AM don't commit infidelity; people do, but those platforms make it a lot easier and even give it some cultural respectability. The media *is* the message, as the saying goes, and the potential for infidelity is woven into the fabric of the technology more than we think. It's what Katherine Hertlein, a professor who studies the impact of technology on relationships, calls the "AAA engine" that drives Internet-based adultery: a computer is accessible, affordable and it offers anonymity. "It's not just that you're communicating with someone online" but that "there is a sexual or emotional nature" in it. The year before last summer's hack, in an *Atlantic* piece on cheating apps, "The Adultery Arms Race," Michelle Cottle argued that technology has made cheating "easier than ever." Though the roots of infidelity have been "more or less constant (the desire for novelty, attention, affirmation, a lover with tighter glutes …), technology is radically altering how we enter into, conduct, and even define it." The convergence of sex and tech allows a private life to morph into a secret one, which is always dangerous because of the intimacy online communication enables. A few months after the AM hack, in an October 2015 *Marie Claire* essay, Deborah Circurel said the computer "is to blame for making cheating not only easier, but also more addictive than ever," which sounds right to me. In an age of digitally driven intimacy disorders, Facebook cheating and emotional infidelity, nothing says suspicion like a spouse's obsessively password-protected iPhone—or her habit of taking it to the bathroom, or his insistence on positioning his laptop so the screen always faces away from you, and so on.

It was a new experience to me—not the philandering but the social network that made it possible—but the thrill of covert carnality made it hard to see that AM wasn't just a window to the theatre of married people's sexuality but more like a door that opened directly to the stage. The first thing you notice is that there are masses of men on the hunt for comparatively few women. AM *is* a woman's market, and the simple discrepancy in demand and supply made for an intensely cavalier attitude among some of its women members. "Men may have discovered fire," says Candace Bushnell, the genius pop-scribbler behind *Sex and the City*, "but women discovered how to play with it." Maybe playing on AM was a third-wave feminist inversion of the power imbalance women experienced offline for the first few thousand years of civilization. Whatever the case, it sometimes seemed like some of them regarded their infidelity superciliously and in magnanimous terms. Katie Roiphe wrote a controversial essay in the *New York Times*, "Adultery: The Double Standard," in which she pointed out the hypocrisy of a culture that treats male infidelity as "a threat to the family," whereas female infidelity "has become a titillating form of self-expression." Women cheat, in short, for historically understandable reasons, but guys cheat because they think with their dicks. Sure, the philandering women I met were more eloquent than I expected, but sometimes it felt as if they genuinely thought their motivations for infidelity were more socially and historically vindicated, like some noble exercise in the liberation of their gender, even if their aim was for pure carnality.

One was a photographer whose profile included so many indiscrete pictures—of herself, mostly, but also of herself with her spouse and children—that it seemed like she didn't care if she got caught. She was a nice woman with a pronounced libido that she said was the result of her frustration with her husband's long work hours, a theme as common among AM women as death at the end of a Shakespeare tragedy. The brunette, a striking Machiavellian with a background in literature, who told me about the fictions she concocted for her husband—whose work-related travel lead to their empty sex life—so he wouldn't get suspicious if he happened to notice the babyseat in the back of their SUV was removed, which she sometimes did just in case one of her meetings intensified into something that couldn't wait for a hotel room. The talkative one who lived platonically with her older husband and who talked about their gardening projects and even gave me a cutting from a hybrid plum tree. Her conversations were so punctuated with sumptuous metaphors that it was hard to tell if she was talking about nourishing gardens or genitalia.

"The first breath of adultery," John Updike writes in *Couples*, "is the freest," and he's right, or at least that was the case in one encounter that turned into an epic narrative. What started as long emails, with their built-in plots of incumbent intimacy, increased slowly and by degrees became a pattern, a ritual of reading messages every morning and responding before noon, repeated in the evenings, and soon enough that pattern morphed, predictably and logically by all accounts of narrative structure with which I'm familiar, into more consistent forms of non-textual contact. It was like walking out of abstraction into sense perception. After a few weeks we started meeting for four to six hours every second Friday afternoon. Those were among the very best days, I'd have to say, filled as they were with smiling and pleasure, and—wretchedly, as such things go—all of them happened because of the secrets and lies we told our spouses. But then adultery is always beyond good and evil, isn't it? Once the door closes, morality is as inconsequential as logic at a mass or condoms in porn. In simple terms, it was as if that overpowering anticipatory rush you get when kissing new lips, wondering about their texture and the degree of gentleness or firmness with which they'll kiss you back, was prolonged over hours and weeks, then months. Like Alistair and Chiara, two characters from a story in Tim Parks's *Adultery and Other Diversions* who'd meet at academic conferences around Europe and have really good, cathartic sex, we did the same but in less exotic locations. After a time of privation in married life, the appetites can only push themselves into an ecstatic reservoir of sensuality that, over the months, went from a long-form fling to a storybook affair saturated in nerves and sweaty lust. She somehow made my loneliness respectable by reducing the guilt I had over a surge in passion that I thought I might never, as a result of nature and time, experience again. We started meeting earlier, in the late mornings, to shop for the day's provisions and then, after those licentious parentheses of time, late in the afternoons or early in the evenings, when the air had the scent of wine, cheese, bread and spent pillow talk, we'd go our separate ways to enjoy the domestic lives with our spouses and families that were adjacent to the secret one that was capable of taking place between us. It felt so European, like a Buñuel film with Catherine Deneuve, so indispensable because sexual adventure won't be denied by fragile moralities, and naturally so wrong because it was so basely biological.

Yet for all its carnality it was a perfectly literary affair, which might be the case with all relationships where the desire for someone—or some*thing*?—else is, like a metaphor standing for an intricate idea in a poem, a vibrant substitution for maybe some narcissistic need or a rough patch in the narrative of your life. An affair isn't motel-room fucking. Well, yes, it is that, literally, but it's also the accelerating allegory of longing, consummation and separation that doubles back to the longing, over and over, and is contained in an alcove of secrecy. The cycle builds anticipation, the narcotic fulcrum that keeps an affair in place and differentiates it from marriage, and the anticipation leads to clandestine words, thousands of messages exchanged in the interstitial time and space between Fridays, and eventually many other days, too. Messages first exchanged on AM shifted to emails and Google chats, and then the occasional surreptitious phone call or text ignored when you're at the dinner table but answered later—*any* language, written or spoken, would mitigate her absence and make it a presence.

And where there are words, there is life and drama. Even now, a decade later, in my mind it's a secretive language game that, like all erotic memories, hangs there like residual threads of fragments that can only become narrative when stitched together with words and sentences. Like adultery, literary language is publically disavowed but secretly practised, and secrets, especially the shameful ones we're not really ashamed of, aren't incommunicable truths of one's being; they exist only because we have language, and this is why secrets can only ever mean something when told, which of course means that secrets always end.

Lovers are the people you tell your secrets too, it's true, but as that clever Frenchman Jean Baudrillard pointed out, "If you say, 'I love you,' then you have already fallen in love with language, which is already a form of break-up and infidelity." Once the alcove of the two-way language game frays, it's the end of the affair. Mine ended when I learned, accidentally, that the secret between us wasn't just a secret between us at all but was, as part of a midlife reawakening on her part, regularly shared across a corner of the sexualized Web that was, in effect, a marketing adjunct to AM. She was a sex blogger, prolific and popular as a result of her fluency in writing about the fine details of her sex-obsessed and brazenly promiscuous year of infidelity on AM for her readers, most of whom seemed to be middle-class types who had enough free time in their lives to spend hours a day sharing stories of their own adulteries, with the occasional racy photo to give them a pornographic edge, for the purpose of community building and, presumably, mutual arousal. I didn't find out for a year and only after I mentioned that I wanted to write a piece on the then still-new AM platform—that's why I went to the site in the first place, though I clearly failed as an impartial observer—and she became apprehensive. I referred to the names of some people I wanted to contact, and she knew of some, she said, like this man from LA who fancied himself a libertine but was a run-of-the-mill libertarian who ran a sex blog called "Ashley and Me" under the banner "Yeah, I'm the guy who's been banging your wife. Sorry." As an affiliate of AM he wrote stories about the women he slept with via AM, and was compensated for referring people to the AM site during its peak years—think of an older, equally arrogant but stately version of the contemporary "pick-up artist" Roosh V—until a "friend" who frequented the same corner of the infidelity world contacted his wife and told her about his secret sex industry. In any case, later that night, after our conversation about the writing project I never started, I clicked around, came across comments on an AM affiliate that seemed familiar, in style and tone, and a few screens later I found myself reading stories about myself and those Friday meetings, well-written and structured with a journalist's eye for disclosing personal, social and even intimate familial details.

I was fictionalized, in other words, rendered a character in her stories, along with all her other AM encounters that year. Which sounds a lot worse than it was because, really, anybody who wants to make their life feel like literature must know that shrapnel and pain always make for better stories. Unhappiness is always easier to write about because in misery, as Graham Greene wrote in *The End of the Affair*, "we seem aware of our own existence, even though it may be in the form of a monstrous egotism." And that was it—my monstrous egotism. And though it hurt, there was something comical about it. Like in Christopher Nolan's film *Inception*, in which you're never sure how to separate "real" from "fantasy" from "fiction," or how to factor in the "meta" levels required to straighten out the plot in your head, there was a reflexive or postmodern irony at work. I set out to write about the culture of online adultery, didn't write about it but did the adultery in the first-person, lived in that secret literary alcove for a year and then, at the end, read about it from the point of view of an author who was an actor in my real life and a character in my represented narrative.

The episode reminded me, some years later, of Edgar Allen Poe's enigmatic story, "The Purloined Letter," in which the queen of France is reading a letter when her husband walks in. She wants to hide it from him—there's something juicy in it, maybe infidelity—but she can't, because that would make her look guilty, so she leaves it on her table, address showing. A conniving minister walks in, notices the letter and the queen's nervousness and steals the letter, replacing it with another, which she notices though she can't say anything about it, because she'd incriminate herself in front of the king. We never learn the content of the letter; we just know it's important, probably scandalous, and that it needs to be kept secret. And it is kept secret because though a detective ultimately finds it, readers never actually learn what it's about. It's a virtuoso work of dramatic plot structure and character motivation, both determined by the literary value of the secret, which years after it was published prompted the psychoanalyst, Jacques Lacan, to call the letter in the Poe story a "pure signifier." That letter is not only like the secret of online adultery I lived for a year, but it's like the secret of adultery, or maybe all sexuality, in its entirety. "What is peculiar to modern societies," according to that other clever Frenchman, Michel Foucault, "is not that they consigned sex to a shadow existence, but that they dedicated themselves to speaking of it *ad infinitum*, while exploiting it as *the* secret."

That Tuesday last summer as we watched the CNN story at the clinic my mother said to me that it was sad those people were shamed for something that was, in the end, so trivial. Not that she condoned the behaviour. Structurally speaking, infidelity is no more wrong than orgasms or breathing or nightfall can be wrong; it's just that that raw state of nature that it represents can't easily fit into the matrix of a rule-bound civilization, even if it makes for dynamic literature and literary alcoves in real life. Adultery, even the ones the AM hack exposed, isn't really ever about adultery; it's about the necessity and impossibility of secrets and the dynamic struggle between, on the one hand, needing to keep them and, on the other, needing to share them. Secretly, we live in a world where adultery and other "shameful" acts exist, but their shamefulness is only a problem when the content escapes its secrecy and becomes public, as all things of language eventually do.

Waiting for the Catastrophe of My Life to Be Beautiful

Human time does not turn in a circle; it runs ahead in a straight line.
That is why man cannot be happy: happiness is the
longing for repetition.

—Milan Kundera, The Unbearable Lightness of Being

I got an unexpected text message from a friend one evening in early December. I was at my desk wondering how to massage a bunch of sentences and partial paragraphs into an essay—*this* essay—on happiness. I wanted to call it "Waiting for the Catastrophe of My Personality to Seem Beautiful Again," an unoriginal title I pulled out of a poem I like, and I wanted it to be just as light and insightful as that poem. In it I planned to write about the happiest and saddest time in my life, which I imagined some people might like to read about.

It was two summers ago, and I accidentally went into a coma while sitting in the kitchen of my East Van home on Father's Day. I woke up the next month and found that the tectonic plates of my world had collided. I almost died, they told me, and part of me I know did, though that was far from the worst part. The tremors were really the result of my own vanity and ego, but because I wanted this piece to be more melodramatic than maudlin, I planned to write about how all that damage and hurt had a good deal to do with the green-eyed acrimony and slanderous hysterics of a woman I called Voldemort.

I never wrote that essay. I might, but for now the prospect of writing about happiness when the narrative involves broken characters, the recalibration of emotional deposits across the quiet desperation of their lives, secretive intrigues and exposed anguish that forever closes some relationships and starts new ones, the impotent ritual of goodbyes, and the malignancy of a casual encounter with mortality is just too bewildering. Like laughing when you've cut yourself badly or whistling in a graveyard at night. But then maybe, like Cormac McCarthy says in *Blood Meridian*, the high point of a guy's life, the meridian, "is at once his darkening and the evening of his day." Yes, it probably is.

So I was at my desk considering all this when my iPhone lit up. The message asks, innocuously, "How are you?" I texted back that I'd been listening to black metal, trying not to lose my mind from all the term papers I'd been marking, and then I answered her question, "I'm all right. Hope you are too." You know how sometimes you're chattering inane pleasantries when the other person says something that makes you aware of just how inane those pleasantries are? Well, it was there, in that awareness and in the minute or two it took my correspondent to type the next installment of dialogue, that our friendship essentially happened.

"I'm a bit fucked up at the moment," she wrote. "How does one carry on with a life that appears to be so rich and so full at the same time as one's interior being is in some sheer crisis about how to live rightly?" Maybe my iPhone didn't really change *everything*, like Apple says in those clever commercials, but that message, pitched at me with the sonorous elegance of a surprise question on a philosophy mid-term you thought was going to be multiple choice, was lacerated with the metaphysical thrum of that proverbial voice of one who cries out from the wilderness.

Milan Kundera has this line in *The Unbearable Lightness of Being*, a novel I've always thought of as a poem dressed up like an essay on human aesthetics, where he says that the brain has a special part that records all the things that charm us and make our lives beautiful. Well, that message charmed its way straight into my "poetic memory." I suppose most of these moments in our lives are attached to lovers, the ones we tell our secrets to, or perhaps to our spouses or children or dogs; but here was my collegial friend, who probably hadn't even been drinking at the time, asking me a question that was so fragile that its words and syntax anchored themselves into that part of my brain that makes life beautiful.

Text messaging, I realize, isn't the best way to address someone's dark night of the soul. I index-fingered some clichéd lines— "Oh, sorry to..." and "I'm sure it'll get..."—then backspaced them out of existence. What does a tragicomic middle-aged guy who spends too much time in his office—and, on that moderately alcohol-fuelled evening, trying not to despise himself too much while wondering why his own happiness and the happiness he was supposed to be writing about was so elusive—say when he gets such a bereaved question from somebody he's always considered a consummate person—a writer, parent, partner, and teacher—who seems to have brilliantly spanned that existential cleavage between soul and self that infects his own and, I'm guessing, so many other lives.

When I'm confronted with the unhappiness that comes from the realization that the lives we're living are malignant dramas of selective truths and lying poses we throw up to maintain the narratives and settings in which we've elected to act—whether they're my own or belong to others—I think of Kundera's novel, which I've read often but finished only once because I dawdle and loiter in too many of his paragraphs. It's therapy; it's my happy place. I used to think the lyrical modulation of the words in the title—*The Unbearable Lightness of Being*—was an all-purpose salve for the serene pain and absurdities of life. If I felt sad or melancholic or lonely I'd pull the title into my head where I imagined it could answer my really big questions with the aplomb of God or Google, even if I didn't know what those questions were.

Recently I've been taken, as if by some magnetic force of syntax that's aligned itself with the turbulent narrative of my life—and, it seems, with the lives of so many other people—to one particular clause. It's where Kundera's staggeringly intellectual narrator, at the beginning of that beautiful love story between Teresa and Tomas, restates Nietzsche's principle of eternal return, which is really the preoccupation of the entire novel: "happiness is the longing for repetition." Like a fate tune that you imagine has been sung just for you, the clause has worked itself into my life—moving from the enchantment of youth to love and marriage and then to its poignant dissolution and now towards a degree of respectable survival—and now, finally, I think I've come close to understanding what it means.

Happiness, if it exists as something more or less tangible, must be in the submicroscopic moments when we give our attention to a soul because that soul has sought us out. It could be the soul of a lover or child or parent or, in my case, a friend. There was a question, and questions always demand answers, but when answers are unavailable, the only responsibility we have is to offer some response.

I considered replying to my friend's "fucked up" question with the truth. *I'm having a hell of a time cataloguing my own existential disintegration. I'm more than halfway through my life and I have no idea what I'm doing.* Or more simply, *I messed things up pretty good when I was asking that same question a couple of years ago, so I'm really not the one to ask.* I even considered reversing the onus and laying down some pathos. *Hey, I had a vacation in unconsciousness where the angel of death had me by the ear and pulled me to the abyss and wouldn't let me close my eyes until he was satisfied that I abandoned all hope.* But that kind of narcissistic subjective slush, no matter how truthful, would make me look like I wasn't wearing big-boy pants. Or too melancholic, and I've always pictured melancholy as an emo-infused dominatrix who goes around pretending to be a doe-eyed Japanimated Lolita who really wants to talk about her problems and never listen to others.

Last year a UBC study concluded that men who display too much happiness might, in fact, finish last. Rating the appeal of people "engaged in universal displays of happiness"—like smiling—that study, which was published in the American Psychological Association journal *Emotion*, questioned whether or not the presumed goodness of being friendly in social contexts is good in interpersonal communication. With guys, apparently, happiness isn't. When I read it I felt vindicated in my own recalcitrant sadness, but that wasn't going to be much help to my friend. Nor would it be helpful if I quoted another study I came across in my obsession with sorting out the impossibility of my own happiness—the Mappiness Project, sponsored by the London School of Economics—that said, after sex and exercise, people are happiest when engaged in artistic pursuits like watching plays and going to museums.

Staring down at the tiny blinking cursor in that empty bar

above my miniature keypad that evening I was somewhat spell-bound because I was taken into a confidence. There's a line in an Al Purdy poem that is one of the most painful things I've ever read. It's one of those pull quotes that you can apply to lots of different situations, kind of like a bit of duct tape for the poignan-cies of life. "I have seen myself fade from a woman's eyes while I was standing there and the earth was aware of me no longer." It's a romantic context, and the poem is about the impermanence of history, and this might not exactly apply in this case, but the sentiment does. Before typing in my response I felt like I had changed souls and the world was aware of me again.

Whether it's with a wife or lover or child, nothing is quite as agonizing as exposing your soul with all its strengths and weak-nesses, virtues and vanities, and nothing is quite as joyful as someone who displays their soul for you.

But questions still warrant replies even if there are no legiti-mate answers. "If I knew what to say to you I'd a told myself the same thing last year and fixed myself. My answer? Spend time in the woods, be helpful to people, beer, listen to the Undertones." That's what I said in my response. Looking back at it now, it seems inane, but it sounded a lot more heroic and even poetic at the time.

I've since wondered if that crisis message—which I read while I was struggling with my own crisis—was an ironic synchronicity that the gods, with all their horoscopical retrogrades and mercu-rial transits, decided to toss at me for their amusement. I mean, is there a better way to remedy the spells of despair in your own life than hearing about a more articulate friend's despair? It's text-book schadenfreude, but if that person reaches out to you—*to me*?—in a moment of unvarnished sodality, then maybe it's just an act of absolute goodness. It's beauty, and happiness, something like the Buddhists mean when they talk about "loving kindness," and it has everything to do with the slowness of conscientious communication with another person who has put you in a state of grace by confiding in you a wound in their life.

Because I'd been teetering on the brink of my own despair ever since I disappeared into a parenthesis for a few weeks of my life two years before I'd done some anecdotal research into the state of my own happiness. To the point that it was, and probably still is, an absurd obsession. I got the "gottaFeeling" app, which I tell people I downloaded because I read about it in the *Financial Times* and because its homepage features a quote from the linguistic-minded Enlightenment philosopher Baruch Spinoza: "Emotion, which is suffering, ceases to be suffering as soon as we form a clear and precise picture of it."

To help me form a picture of my suffering, every day for half a year my iPhone's been pinging me, usually in mid-afternoon, and asking "How do you feel?" The possibilities go from "Happy" to "Guilty/Shame." Earlier that afternoon in December when I got the message, I clicked the first, and it asked "What level of Happy do you feel?" "Jovial," I thought and pressed, but only because classes were done for the term and I'd already had a couple of drinks. After I registered my feeling, the screen repeated "You feel jovial," which I already knew, and showed me a pleasant black-and-white cartoon sketch of a woman who looks like Olive Oyl drinking a glass of wine and sitting on a chair in a field with nothing but a hill and some trees in the background.

When I'm feeling "Guilty," the worst feeling you can have on the gottaFeeling app, and I register the level of guilt as "Mortified," the screen shows me a despondent woman, her back towards me and hands in her pockets—although she should probably have a drink in one of them—sulking away in the direction of her long shadow. I've seen that picture often in the last half year, although I'm not at all sure how picturing this or any of the other feelings has eased my suffering, or even if this simplified iconic representation is what Spinoza had in mind with his line about forming a "clear and precise picture" of suffering.

The same day I got my friend's text message I also did an online chakra test. I noticed it in the advertisement bar at the top of my Gmail inbox. I'm not exactly sure what sort of thing a chakra is, but my results sounded pretty bad. All of them were "closed," except for my heart chakra, which the online test told me was "weak." The "Chakra Healing Team" has been kind enough to send me at least one remedy a day since I've been doing the test. I'm not sure if it's helped, but it probably doesn't hurt, right?

I've tried many things to eliminate the chasm that separates who I am from who I appear to be—to be happy—and alleviate the resulting sadness that comes from not being able, ultimately, to do it. Buddhism, yoga, herbs, sex, increasing my quotient of Facebook friends and "Liking" their stuff in the hopes that they'd like mine back, narcotics, psyllium, running farther, reading, drinking more, moving into an office with a better view, wearing clothes more suitable to a college English prof, bird watching, punishing myself with guilt for the hurt I've caused others, tending to plants, quality time with my daughter and dogs. I even tried therapy, but my employer covers only part of the cost, and I can't afford that kind of counselling bling to give the inside of my head a makeover.

But in that momentary exchange with my friend, which I'm sure to anybody else seems entirely unremarkable, there *was* a happiness. It happened between the expression of vulnerability that came in the form of a text message that evening in early December and a hesitant, inelegant response. That's where happiness is, I think, and maybe that's the only place it can ever be. In the agonizing slowness that happens inside you when you're considering another person's wounds.

Andre Dubus, the New England writer of extraordinary midlife-crisis and disintegrating-relationship novellas, says in *We Don't Live Here Anymore*, that what kills a marriage faster than adultery is the selective dialoguing that comes with it. There are always things, in other words, that the two people can no longer talk about—love, desire, intimacy, passion—and that's the problem: "You avoid touching wounds and therefore avoid touching the heart." Many of us know this first-hand about our relationships, but maybe not so much about touching hearts in contexts outside of marriage. How can you ever be happy when you don't touch hearts and, when necessary, wounds? Not to heal them, just to acknowledge that they're there.

Say What You See in the Dark

Throw away the light, the definitions,
And say what you see in the dark.

—Wallace Stevens, "The Man with the Blue Guitar"

I can't imagine anybody wanting to read this, aside from health-care professionals who are curious about unscientific expositions on consciousness disorders, people who have experienced one of these shadowy mental states, or those who just like reading about the maddening psychological traumas of other people. For three weeks in 2010 I was in a medically induced coma because my lungs, as a result of a couple bouts of pneumonia and my own idiocy, couldn't remove enough of the carbon dioxide my body produced. Respiratory acidosis is what the doctors call it, and it happens when all the excess CO_2 causes the pH of your blood and other body fluids to decrease, making them too acidic. The coma, which kept me from certain death, was an eventful paren-thesis in my conscious life, filled as it was with sadistic nightmares and hellish scenes on par with Dante, Milton and Wes Craven. There were five scenes, kind of like a five-act tragedy but far less structured, that recursively looped through my mind while I was comatose and also since that time. I jotted down these fragments and surreal vignettes shortly after I was released from the hospital because my brain wanted to grasp at some form of narrative or-ganization, but more recently, long after the fact, I came back to them because it occurred to me that I hadn't had a decent night-mare, or even a good dream for that matter, since the coma.

Maybe I do dream but just forget, I don't know, but it's almost as if a part of my consciousness—the dramatic part responsible for the nightmares and dreams—has gone missing, or maybe it was just outdone by those five recursive vignettes. But then consciousness is not a thing at all but is a noun that sometimes doubles as a verb, and at its clearest edge is blurred by adjectives and adverbs and everywhere secured with the other parts of speech. "The word alone," the philosopher Heidegger once said, "gives being to the thing," but if the word is as dim as this one, then what kind of "being" is it?

The abyss of Act I starts at night, and there's music, which activates the lights, eight of them on the ceiling, their beams tracking down across the farthest wall in a methodical *dance macabre* that marks, for lack of an explanation that's inside logic, a burlesque ritual of regimented torture and a mocking parade of imminent death. Most of the songs I don't know—neither the names nor the artists, or it could be that I just can't name them—but some I do, like the climactic one in the repertoire, which repeats itself early every evening or late afternoon or every few hours or whenever all the other lights on the second floor go out and my feet are flayed, cut into five slivers of parboiled flesh and cartilage. It's a track from the film *Hanna*, a Chemical Brothers song called "The Devil Is in the Details," which the blonde sadistic character of ambiguous sexuality whistles with ominous precision. But this isn't possible, because the movie comes out next year, yet it must be possible because what I know for sure is that this song means my feet will be sliced from the tops, the dorsum pedis, through to the sole, starting with an incision in the tender skin between the toes and moving down across the tops, through the tendons, in the direction of the heel by eight razor beams of light.

A lead guitar tuned to sound like a muted whistle carries the melody, barely perceptible drumming and a rhythmic base that gets faster and louder but increases neither in speed nor volume, and the track lights oscillate slowly like the ink jets on a dot-matrix printer, not to the music but in a consistent pattern devised by some unseen psychopath who wants to punish me. Eight white bulbs or spotlights, I don't know which, because they're discreet and formally focused, much like a simple table lamp next to a con-dolence book at a funeral home, housed in moveable frames hinged to a four-foot track on the ceiling perpendicular to my body. The song starts sounding like rockabilly cabaret, and the razor beams, which when stationary are always aimed at the top of the wall that's closest to the foot of the bed, the penumbra casting par-allel strips of shadowy light across the ceiling in the oblique man-ner of venetian blinds in a film noir, cast points of light down the wall with the slow sweep of a pendulum, sometimes seeming to stop and sweep back the other way in mock reprieve, before con-tinuing down to my feet, which they will slice open.

I watch the eight points vine down the wall as if on their own volition, closer over the bed frame, and when they reach the longest toes on both feet, which are splayed outward like when you're sleeping or dead, they become flares tipped with a single bevelled edge. It smoulders at first like the carburizing flame of a welder's torch, but when it glows, it narrows. Each tip makes an incision between my toes where the skin is as susceptible as a jugular. The sensation is shrill and impeccable, like cutting the inside of your finger with a sashimi knife, which is made for carving raw flesh without destroying the beauty of its organic structure; not just a cut but a slice, thin and piercing, which seizes your finger and then your whole hand with that screaming

tension of evacuating blood, the pain throbbing with a pornographic rawness that leaves you embarrassed at being a body
that's so vulnerable and irrelevant. "Everybody is a book of
blood," as horror master Clive Barker says, "wherever we're
opened, we're red."

I'd avoid the pain if I could, but my ankles, like my wrists, are
strapped. A few times after the first punishments I managed to
outwit the engineers of my captivity by determining the arc of
each light, gauging its movement with the soundtrack and considering the angles at which each point descends the wall to the
foot of the bed and at which moment, at which precise second,
each reaches my feet for the slicing. And twice, maybe three
times, I recognized a pattern, so I contorted my legs and feet, extending my toes in an intentional spasm, and that way I avoided
a few incisions. It turns out that if any of the razor light beams
didn't make contact with the midpoint between the toes, then
the corresponding light source on the ceiling would go out, and
I'd be one spared that cut. Mostly, though, I watched the eight
points cross the ceiling and sink down the wall to slice my feet
into fifths. Four cuts on each foot, executed with a Japanese
chef's precision in preparing pufferfish, five portions insanely
parallel and clinically executed with minimal blood. Imagine
someone taking a razor, eight of them, one for the space between each of your toes, placing it so the cold edge just touches
the prone skin, and then slowly, in the unhurried orchestral
movements of a cellist manoeuvring his bow, slice through flesh
down in the direction of your heel. Sometimes, presumably to
pre-empt me from recognizing the pattern of the lights and dis-
rupting the cuts, the beams would appear on my knees and shins
first, and I'd watch, surprised and unprepared, as they'd move

over my skin or the mess of bed sheets over my legs, searing and cutting me into fifths down to my heels, always to the same song. It's repetitive, like a TV crime show you know very well but not well enough to anticipate the moves in its plot.

I'd look down over the ventilation thing they shoved down my throat and secured over my mouth and nostrils, past the IV lines and the catheter and the other tubes and rubber lines securing me to "a state of unrousable unconsciousness"—which is how the *Oxford Medical Dictionary* defines "coma"—but keeping me a few degrees from brain death, and I'd see those equal portions of meat dangling there, at the ends of those cartilage and skin stems sprouting from my heels, all ten toes still at their tips, where my whole feet used to be and I'd cry, inaudibly, physically helpless because I'd never walk again and psychologically unhinged because someone was fucking up my feet for no other reason than to see if he could do it. I imagine the anticipation of surgery before the years of anesthesia must have instilled this kind of terror in people, this expectation of inescapable pain meted out with such regularity that—like the infernal symmetry of a water faucet dripping at night in a distant room or a clock ticking—the consistency of the predictable pattern ties the pause to the execution. It's like the fear struck by that famous image from that surrealist film by Salvador Dali and Luis Buñuel, *Un Chien Andalou,* which opens with a man sharpening a razor and soon cuts to a shot of a woman sitting and calmly staring at us as he slits her eye with the blade; the gelatinous vitreous ooze drips from her eyeball, which is gross but never as terrifying as the anticipation of that razor slice to the eye at the establishing shot.

I'd drift off to sleep and when I'd wake, still asleep, my feet were whole again, but the soundtrack would start soon enough, every few hours or every afternoon or evening. I don't know exactly how often any of this happened though I know it *did* happen, though not in the empirical sense of an "experience" that can be represented by any words or sentences. Consciousness, that weird spatial, neurological fiction we circumscribe with a noun whose etymology takes it to the Latin word *conscius*, a compound of *con* or "together" and *scio* or "to know," is a malleable metaphor that designates a thing but which has a sense of time at its edges that makes it impossible to understand, especially when you're talking about your own consciousness, which you experienced as a set of surreal hallucinations that happened to you only on the stage of your own mind, and doubly impossible to narrate.

So, too, were the other four acts in my coma drama—like the serialized theatre of cruelty performed on my family, more predictable even than the razor sadism but with the same anguished endpoint. My point of view doesn't change, but this time I'm in the pit of something like Shakespeare's theatre, the Globe, in London—where I've never been—looking up from the bed where I'm unconscious with my eyes closed, and I see my family acting, but they don't know they're on stage. The word I could have used at the time is uncanny, *unheimlich* as Freud and my mother would say in the indisputably true Germanic accent of psychoanalysis, but I couldn't say it at the time and so I couldn't think it, either. Less a stage than a series of balconies linked behind the backdrop, different hallways groping their way horizontally, in and out of the wall, beyond the foot of my bed. Had I been conscious and able to speak, I'd say it gave me the illusion of the famous eighteenth-century architect, Piranesi, whose fictitious 1750 etchings for prisons, *Carceri*, inspired the gothic part of Romanticism fifty years later and Surrealism a hundred and some years after that; it gave me a perspective similar to watching the glockenspiel at Marienplatz in Munich chime at 11 a.m. and perform its stories on those split levels. The characters—my mother, my niece, and for some reason just a shadow trace of my daughter—are wooden figurines fashioned in the Black Forest—where, like Marienplatz in Munich, I have been—but they don't re-enact the dramas about a sixteenth-century Bavarian duke or the dancing barrel makers. They walk in a line, my mother walking right to left with purpose ahead of her two grandchildren, along the balconies cropping out of the wall. They come out of the balcony doors and move along, sometime talking about whether or not they are lost, and they'd disappear behind the wall into the adjacent door on the left. They're here to visit me, I know this, but they're led astray, always imprisoned, and on a few times they're executed in front of me, placed in cupboards whose walls compress and squeeze them, and I can hear the first shouts of indignation evolve into hideous screams because each cupboard has a barred window, and the man responsible is the same diabolical sadist who slices my feet. I'm bound and immobile and I can't save them and they are calling me. Like that scene in *The Wizard of Oz* in which Dorothy is crying in the tower, "I'm frightened, Auntie Em," and then her aunt appears in the crystal ball calling out for her niece just as a mother might do, but then that momentary consolation fades and is replaced with the Wicked Witch who is laughing hysterically.

Above me the track lighting elongating my toes at regular intervals, a wall in front of me that's a macabre cuckoo clock torturing two and a half of my family members at more irregular intervals, neither of which were real, and below me something equally delirious. Act III. The floor is in rotating geometrical motion. Patterned black-and-white checkered tiles to my left—I never looked right; I don't know why—that resembled a horizontal Tetris game that curved up the walls with no exit in sight except for a hallway that circled back in on itself, and it all looked like I was being wrapped in a *New York Times* cryptic crossword. The tiles would shift by some loosely defined linear logic, move laterally across the floor, one at a time, in one of four directions, and as a consequence push all the others this way and that to accommodate the movement. Now and then, one of them would elevate, announce itself with a brighter light, flip over and become its opposite, white to black and black to white, which would alter each of the other squares in a domino pattern. But, in a nightmarish twist of the old fable about the peasant who asks an ancient shah in Persia to give him a single grain of rice on a chessboard square and double it progressively until the eight-by-eight board is covered in rice, when a person appeared on the floor there would be another square added, which rendered the system an exponential nightmare. As Carl Sagan once said, "Exponentials can't go on forever, because they will gobble up everything." On top of all that impossible geometry, if there happened to be a person standing on the third of a consecutive sequence of black or white squares, if even for a second while they were shifting colour, that person would be pulled into the floor, eliminated. As with the lights and the theatre of the walls, I spent minutes or weeks laying there, head tilted left trying to determine which square would disappear, and when my wife came to visit me—which she really did—I was terrified that she'd be swallowed up, and I told her so, loudly and aggressively, or so she said after; I'd demand that she move, that the squares were about to shift and she would be displaced into the floor. And once I remember she was pulled down, and in her place was a nurse with dark hair sitting at a little desk on wheels that looked like a guardhouse in purgatory. I remember well my wife's voice, though I was unconscious and unrousable, because she has one of the most calming voices I've ever heard. This third act in my fucked-up head-drama is still, all these years after my coma, the source of an occasional joke about my obviously still brain-damaged condition that my now ex-wife shares in those adorable moments of black humour, which at least is testament that some of my "hallucinations" while comatose were not exclusively fantasies but had some expression in language, though of course none of the others—neither my ex nor the nurse at that infernal desk or any of the others—could see what I meant when I told them to move so the floor didn't consume them.

On September 21, 1939, at the age of eighty-three, Sigmund Freud slipped into a coma as a result of an injection of three large doses of morphine. I don't know if he would have said the world he inhabited for those two days before he died on September 23 was the result of involuntary thought processes that satisfied his unconscious desires by coding them as metaphors, though in his waking life he did say that dreams are such distorted "wish-fulfil-ments." Unlike Freud, I didn't die, and I'm pretty sure my ugly nightmares weren't just veiled figures that I could trace back along metaphorical lines to some literal desire of my ego or superego. I wouldn't even say they were anxiety dreams, which Freud be-lieved were the dreams least distorted by coded metaphors. They were nightmares enacted and experienced in the oblivion of my real-life coma, and they were sublimely terrible in some other-worldly manner that caught me off guard. The word "nightmare" in its current use has a short history, dating back not more than a few hundred years. Samuel Johnson, who compiled the first exhaustive dictionary of the English language in 1755, defined "nightmare" as a kind of sleep paralysis: "a morbid oppression during sleep, resembling the pressure of weight upon the breast." Before Johnson's time nightmares were thought to be the work of demons, usually a female figure like an incubus, who sits on a person's chest while asleep, which is the personified version of frightening dreams that the old English and Germanic root word "mare" originally signified. There's this famous eighteenth-century painting by Henry Fuseli called *The Nightmare*, in which a woman in white stretches across a bed, sleeping, but there's an ape-like monster crouching on her chest wanting to molest and terrify her. The painting—apparently, Freud had a reproduction hanging in his Vienna office—is a personification of that freak-out condition of sleep paralysis that takes hold of you when you're about to fall asleep and realize, awake in mind but paralyzed in body, that you can't move or speak or cry out.

I imagine the distress of our nightmares is, like the most acute agonies we experience while awake, never the blood and guts or grotesque monsters but the overwhelming carnage of isolation with which we experience them, that sense—or is it a grudging realization?—that, as Orson Welles put it in that famous line, "We're born alone, we live alone, we die alone." That's just a pocket cliché we can rattle of in the maudlin moments of life or when we're drunk or stoned and speaking in metaphysical riddles just to keep the buzz going, but I suspect it's much more than that. Sartre, in one of his quintessentially French moments, famously said that "Hell is—other people," and as much as I get why he'd say this, I also think there's nothing as unbearably odious as the inability or unwillingness to connect to other people. Isolation, loneliness, emotional quarantine: it took me far too long to realize that these are the demonic extremities of dread. "Alone," Stephen King writes, "that's the key word, the most awful word in the English tongue. Murder doesn't hold a candle to it and hell is only a poor synonym." Nightmares are ours and always ours alone, and the difficulty we have in describing them to people corroborates their intense subjectivity. Samuel Beckett, in whose work the term "alone" is a thematic keyword, once wrote with characteristic tragicomic despair, "And you as you always were. Alone." There's a poem by Charles Bukowski, "Love Is a Dog from Hell," that echoes something of the same monstrous sentiment: "there is a loneliness in this world so great / that you can see it in the slow movement of / hands of a clock," he writes, then speaks of "the gutters," "the suicides" and "the terror of one person / aching in one place / alone." Even that busted-up beautiful line in the Bible about "the voice of one crying in the wilderness" points to the agony of isolation.

You'll never be alone if your body, like mine, gives up part of its ghost and you find yourself in a coma, because there are loads of people in the Intensive Care Unit—one nurse stationed with every patient, abundant doctors and specialists, some with residents following them listening to them hold court about your condition, physiotherapists, counsellors, and other uniformed staff flitting about—yet, even though you're unconscious, at some level aware enough of your context that you might pull some of it into your head but probably not enough to make the narrative you weave there into anything more than a hopelessly idiosyncratic inward plot, you couldn't be more alone. Not ever, unless you were dead, but then you'd be dead and couldn't register the loneliness, so never. Certainly not to the extent that all your experiences are so forcibly yours and yours alone, and doubly so because nobody will really believe that these experiences happened to you—even you wouldn't believe it—because of course they didn't happen, not in any believable way that our blurry language of consciousness allows.

The standard definition of the noun "coma," though it derives etymologically from the Greek word κῶμα or *koma*, meaning "deep sleep," is structured in staggeringly binary terms, simple either/or generalizations that don't allow for much nuance. Three doctors in a recent paper on "Brain Function in Coma," which I found in the famous British medical journal, the *Lancet*, define a "coma" as "a state of unresponsiveness" characterized "by the absence of arousal and thus also of consciousness," wherein the patient "has no awareness of self or surroundings," plain and simple. Even the populist and overly simple WebMD, the online go-to source for most of our ailments, says a comatose person "is alive" but "cannot be awakened by any stimulation, including pain." Three different doctors in an influential 2010 paper called "General Anesthesia, Sleep, and Coma," which appeared in the renowned *New England Journal of Medicine* and was even reported in *Scientific American*, defined coma as "a state of profound unresponsiveness" and said comatose patients "lie with eyes closed and cannot be roused to respond appropriately to vigorous stimulation." When I went to the *NEJM* website to look for more work on coma because I wanted to find out exactly what had happened to me during that three-week parenthesis of my life, I learned that the official browse category is "Coma/Brain Death," which is an inauspicious category if you happen to believe you remember parts of your coma. The International Brain Injury Association defines coma as "an acute condition...defined by a complete absence of awareness." I read a recent opinion piece in *Trends in Cognitive Sciences* in which "consciousness" is "described as involving 'a scale ranging from total unconsciousness (e.g., death and coma) to vivid wakefulness.'" Coma and death are often just a spit away from each other on most medical diagrams and graphs, too, when the words aren't enough to impart a definition.

I suppose that's how I looked from the outside for the three weeks I was in a coma. How else would I have looked, wrists and ankles bound with those tubes going in and coming out of me? Nurses and doctors thought I was unconscious, unrousable, unresponsive, and unaware of my surroundings, alive but only to the extent that the wires were registering some vital signs, yet barely removed from brain death, and they were right. But that's not what it *looked* like from the inside, or maybe that's not what it *sounded* and *smelled* like? If there are different circles of Hell, like Dante said there are, then one of those circles must be like coming out of a coma and trying to explain where you were to people who think you'd just taken leave of your consciousness and were hallucinating because of all the pretty fine drugs they give you in the ICU. Dorothy Gale has a comparatively easy time of it when she wakes up and tells Aunt Em, Uncle Henry and Professor Marvel that she really did leave them and had been to Oz.

For a few years after my coma I did what I thought most normal people would do with their disturbing nightmares: I jotted them down into a bullet-point five-act tragedy because I didn't want to forget them—as if I could ever forget them—but besides that I pretty much repressed them, tossed them into the dustbin of my personal history and didn't really talk about them at any

length except for on a couple of occasions, when I told a counsellor the hospital sent to make sure I wasn't cracking up a few
weeks after I was discharged, and then a couple more times a
month later when I found my own psychiatrist because I thought
I was. I was to talk about my "night terrors" to, I suppose, get
control of them or find my balance or something like that by or-
ganizing them with thematic metaphors, build sentences and
then narratives to render the delirious fragments into meaningful
units, and so control them. The thing of it is that it didn't matter
who I told because most people responded with the same
quaintly empathic but basically incredulous look. As if it were a
dream, which it was, and I was a child who'd just awoke to tell
his parent, which I wasn't. And it can be infuriating, even traumatic, to be met with that patronizing response, rather like being
told that a line in a poem you read, a philosophy book you read,
a film you watched, or some event you consider to be one of
those memorably meaningful experiences or epiphanies—"To
see a World in a Grain of Sand / And a Heaven in a Wild Flower
/ Hold Infinity in the palm of your hand / And Eternity in an
hour," as William Blake said—is interesting but just not real and
certainly not of any use.

Some years later someone asked me one morning if I had any
dreams. I hadn't, not the night before, and not really since I was
roused from my induced coma. I got curious and Googled
"coma" and "nightmares" and phrases like "am I crazy or psychotic?" I got a screen jammed with information that caught me
off guard. The counsellor the hospital sent me and the one I saw
a month later may have mentioned something about the
"trauma" of being in a coma, and maybe I read the word
"trauma" in those nice little pamphlets the hospital sent home

with me, but I was floored to learn that a sizeable portion of people who come out of a coma alive experience "post-traumatic stress disorder." I don't like the phrase. PTSD sounds way too serious for the time I was confined to Bed 7 across from that nursing station in ICU, like it should be confined to the disorders suffered by soldiers or people who've experienced violence in the tactile world outside their minds. But whatever we call it, some of the material I found did make me feel vindicated, less demented and certainly less alone than I felt after my coma. A wonderful essay in the *New York Times*, "Nightmares after the ICU," traced the case of a Texas nurse, Lygia Dunsworth, who experienced many of the same kinds of cruel and terrifying scenes when she was intubated and put into a coma. Certain "grim" treatments in the ICU—the feeling of suffocation and speechlessness resulting from a plastic tube shoved down into your windpipe to mechanize breathing, wrist and ankle restraints, invasive catheters, opioids, heavy sedation with delirium-inducing benzodiazepines—the essayist writes, "may raise the odds that a patient develops PTSD." I found an eloquent YouTube video of a man named Anthony Russo, who spoke at a 2013 California medical conference about "ICU Delirium," also in terms of brutal scenes that were familiar to me: "What I don't want to be is defined by what happened to me," he says. "But unfortunately what happened to me sort of has defined a lot of what I am today." I read a piece in the *Skeptical Inquirer* by Stephanie Savage, "Covert Cognition: My So-Called Near-Death Experience." She was in a six-week coma during which her family "noticed signs of [her] increasing awareness, but their observations were disregarded by the doctors." While she was comatose, her boyfriend was at her bedside, and he often talked about their future, which is one of the things family members are instructed to do by ICU nurses, but when she regained consciousness he started telling her the same things, and she "would say, basically, 'Been there; heard that,' albeit through his doppelganger." I even found a website through Vanderbilt University in Nashville, which has operated a post-ICU clinic since 2012. The site offers an exhaustive library of video testimonials and PTSD resources online, like support networks, on its ICU Delirium and Cognitive Impairment Study Group page. I was treated well, medically speaking, but when I gained consciousness, I would have liked to be asked by doctor or nurse what it was like being in the coma, not just how I felt but where I was, and perhaps directed to a place where I didn't feel entirely alone, though of course medical staff are already burdened with all that work.

Even more helpful were the medical-journal papers on matters of consciousness and comatose patients, and they were far less subjective and so more credible than most of the personal anecdotes I came across. The same year I was in a coma, a paper titled "Willful Modulation of Brain Activity in Disorders of Consciousness" appeared in the *NEJM*. It reported that patients who are vegetative—to use that horrible but clinically accurate botanical metaphor—can still respond to external stimuli while in a functional magnetic resonance image machine, which is quite the milestone because it means that a line of communication between patients considered far gone and doctors can be opened up, and naturally a key in determining consciousness is the nature and boundaries of communication itself. The authors, Adrian Owen, a pioneering British neuroscientist who now works and teaches at Western University in London, Ontario, and a bunch of his colleagues, aimed to "harness and nurture any available response ... into a form of reproducible communication" whether "functional verbal or nonverbal." They came up with a method to enable a vegetative patient to answer yes or no to simple questions about family with the use of the fMRI. To answer yes, the patient was told to think of playing tennis, which is a motor activity; and to answer no, was instructed to think of walking around their home, room to room, which creates activity in the spatial awareness part of the brain. The patient provided answers, indicated by a change in blood flow to certain parts of his brain. A few years later, Owen and his team reported on a fMRI study in which a man who'd been in a vegetative state for sixteen years responded with almost the same brain patterns as healthy patients did while watching an episode of the old TV show *Alfred Hitchcock Presents*. The patients were not asked to speak or write but to watch; their corresponding thoughts were registered by changes in blood flow to the brain. The vegetative patient showed patterns of activity in the brain responsible for executive processing—in the episode a child is about to fire a gun at her mother and viewers need to think about how many bullets she loaded in the previous scene, which requires deductive thinking and an understanding of foreshadowing plot devices— just like the healthy subjects, which is important because it proved that occasions of conscious awareness occur even though they'd been previously written off. This means, essentially, that patient was following the suspenseful plot, just like the others. It was, as *Maclean's* magazine reported, "the first time that anyone had exchanged information with someone in a vegetative state." Elsewhere Owen and his colleagues, in "A New Era of Coma and Consciousness Science," argued that fMRI technology might soon become "a form of communication, replacing speech or a motor act in patients for whom such forms of behavioural expression are unavailable." This new nonverbal communication might link patients suffering from disorders of consciousness with doctors, allowing them "to communicate their wishes (e.g. concerning treatment options), and, therefore, to exert their right to autonomy." When I read that, I couldn't help but wonder about the recent Canadian legislation on the matter of doctor-assisted suicide. Owen said in a news item reported by the *Guardian* that all this recent research showed "that the prevailing view" on the levels of "awareness/consciousness" among coma patients, minimally conscious patients, and vegetative patients "is categorically incorrect." Though the research focused on the last category, it is remarkable to think that the metaphors of consciousness and awareness, which we can't live without, are reconsidered because research shows that at least some patients who were previously thought to be completely unconscious are aware of both themselves and their surroundings. This finding raises the issue of communicating with people who are considered shut off from life as we currently understand it.

In a more recent piece Owen and his posse of neurophilosophical colleagues argue that as "the science of consciousness matures," it is "in need of constructs to guide research and theorising." To this end, thinking of consciousness in terms of "levels" isn't ideal because the image of levels suggests that "states of consciousness can be ordered in terms of a single dimension." Like a building with floors or a graph emplotting points along the X and Y axes. A better way, they say, is to consider states of consciousness "as regions in a multidimensional space." I'm no scientist, but what they mean by this is that we need better spatial and topographical metaphors to fully comprehend what consciousness is, especially in light of the recent innovations in the language of fMRI communications. When we speak of consciousness, we sort of think we know what we're talking about, and in a sense we do. Medical people talk about consciousness in terms of two categories, I learned in an essay in the *Lancet*: "arousal" and "awareness." The problem, as the writers explained not too differently from Owen and his crew, is that "consciousness cannot be measured objectively by any machine. Its estimation requires the interpretation of several clinical signs." The fact that consciousness, that blurry metaphor, is a matter of "signs" excites me linguistically because it means that discussions on what kind of thing "consciousness" is are just as much a language game as a neurological one.

I admit that reading about the PTSD accounts in the medical journal papers partly vindicated a thought that's been lingering with me for some time now, which is that what happened in my head during my three-week hiatus from consciousness wasn't a parenthetical set of hallucinations induced by drugs, though drugs played a part. It was a form of consciousness, just a different form, or maybe a different "level," one that has yet to be clinically designated with an unblurry set of metaphors—if that can *ever* be done—and documented in medical dictionaries. An art exhibition called "States of Mind: Tracing the Edges of Consciousness" opened in February 2016 at the Wellcome Collection, a gallery in London, England, and its aim, according to its website, is to "examine perspectives from artists, psychologists, philosophers and neuroscientists to interrogate our understanding of the conscious experience." Adrian Owen's case studies of communication established with allegedly vegetative patients using fMRI are a key part of that show. It is, according to a *New Scientist* story, not an artistically appealing part, just screens

showing simple expositions and the fMRI images, and it even in-
cludes the medical-journal references, but it achieves "something
that people have been trying to do for centuries—it makes
thought visible."

Stephen King wrote that "nightmares exist outside of logic, and
there's little fun to be had in explanations; they're antithetical to
the poetry of fear." And he should know. But I've spent hours
decoding the exquisitely unreasonable nightmares I had during my
three-week parenthesis to prove that, beyond the intense poetry
of the fears they left with me, there must have been some logic
and reason at work in the projection booth of my comatose head,
some literal X, a real event or person or memory or word that
prompted all those sadistic and maniacal vignettes recursively
looping through me. My feet ritually sliced to the "The Devil Is in
the Details"? The only thing I can ground that in is that about a
week before my coma I was pruning back a wildly overgrown
Lady Banks rose bush, which collapsed on my right forearm,
leaving thin, claw-like markings on my unsleeved skin. But then
if my eyes were closed while in the coma, would I have built the
razor-beam torture from a memory of a gardening cut? The
nurses, I heard sometime later, when soliciting patient history from
my wife when she was at my bedside, asked if I was depressed
because the marks made it look like I was a "cutter." I was not,
though rose-thorn scars do look a bit like razor-blade markings.
The glockenspiel Shakespearean drama on the wall? I'm sure that
my wife told me she'd contacted my mother soon after the
ambulance took me from home that Father's Day in 2010 and
delivered me to the ICU, that my daughter and favourite niece send
their best, though I know she wouldn't have told my aging mother
that I was as close to death as I was, for obvious reasons. Beyond

that, images unearthed from childhood and typical mother issues, like on my first day at kindergarten, I apparently wouldn't stop telling the other kids in German that "my mother isn't leaving me here, she's coming back." Was that enough plot material to weave into the theatre of cruelty that repeatedly forced me to watch them being killed? As for the Tetris cryptic-crossword floor that changed colours and disappeared people, I have no idea, other than the exponential growth of the black-and-white patterns was a visual sign for my loss of the sense of time while comatose: I remember when I was initially roused back to "consciousness" that the nurses obsessively asked me what year and month it was, what season and what kind of weather we experienced, and though it felt as though I knew the truth, what came out of my mouth was always wrong. I remember this because this kind of near-aphasia made me angrier with the nurses than I usually was.

The one thing I *did* figure out is that there was some faint logic in these three recurrent nightmares, which I ordered this way only because to my best recollection they first appeared in my mind in this sequence: in the first, I was the only subject being hurt and I didn't speak; in the second, I watched two and a half family members lured, tricked and often murdered but I heard them speaking, though I said nothing to them to warn them, which was as agonizing as it was infuriating; in the third, I exchanged words about that diabolical floor with nurses and my wife, too, which is a fact because she has not only told me about it but has joked about my groundless delirium after the fact. In my mind this sequence imitates in narrative form the progress from unconsciousness to a state of partial consciousness, but then who knows? Maybe the laws of narrative don't apply to patients with disorders of consciousness. The other two nightmares that recursively looped through my mind while I was comatose I haven't written about, and this is mostly because one, Act IV, is the most traumatic memory of that three-week hiatus and it was the most repeated, too, for reasons that I suspect could be connected down the metaphorical landscape of my head to literal life. It involved two nurses, one or both of whom were happily psychotic and clearly sadistic, and the death of a third nurse whom the first two persuaded me to kill and then hide in a storage closet that contained real body parts and theatrical props, some of which also appeared in the glockenspiel drama on the wall. But it also involved a degree of cruelty—violent rapes, dismemberment—that I haven't told anybody about simply because their degree of barbarism has made me fearful of the depravity that's hidden in my soul. (During my second coma two years later, which was shorter in duration and happened for completely different reasons, I remember the nurses were lurid and borderline cruel and pornographic in how they would interact with me, though it was also more comical for some reason, perhaps because one of them, I learned when I regained consciousness, had read *Fifty Shades of Grey*, an inane novel that I had just taught in a literature and marketing class.)

The last nightmare, Act V in my mental drama, was the least recurrent, and it involved a handful of other nurses and a Filipino maintenance man, who took undue pleasure in my discomfort. I would ask them, obsessively, through the various things attached to my mouth and face, when I was going home, and they would assure me I would soon be released from the hospital, and then laugh and dismiss me each time I'd ask when. I also wanted a TV, which they gave me, but it only came with prepackaged episodes of *The Mentalist*, a show I don't think I'd ever seen before that time. In any case, Act V typically closed when I was finally released by way of a helicopter that transported me, still in hospital gear, with tubes and wires sprouting from my body, from VGH west to Vancouver Island for some reason, somewhere close to Nanaimo. But the nurses who came with me opened the door and pushed me out while over the ocean, a few hundred metres from shore. I can think of real prompts that activated both these last two recurrent nightmares, but explaining them isn't for here. As for the pronounced negativity of all five of them, I'd rather not think about that too much; for a time, I convinced myself that this was my mind's way of giving me a taste of the despair and hell I'll have to go through when I die, and though I'm not a very spiritual guy, I'd like to think that the end of life will be an end rather than an extended version of the same theatre of cruelty.

I still don't know what consciousness is, certainly not my own, other than a metaphorically charged noun that can double as a verb and has at its most secure semantic edges a lot of adjectives and adverbs, but I have a better idea of the significance in determining with nuanced precision its various meanings, for theoretical and practical reasons. I don't know why I don't really have nightmares anymore, either, but it could be that I just can't remember them. But if that's the case, then I don't quite understand why I can't. Maybe it's that nothing can compare to the surreal hell of those five acts I experienced while my consciousness was bracketed off? I wasn't dreaming and I wasn't awake but I was straddling both, intermittently conscious and unconscious, rousable and unrousable, maybe like when those ghosts of Christmas come and show Scrooge around, except my ghosts were made of the most toxic, probably the most depraved and sinful parts of my soul. The coma was certainly the most interesting thing that happened in my otherwise mundane life so far.

It's a good conversation piece, though I don't really talk about it much, except in blithe hyperbolic terms, as when I used to tell my kid the first year after being released that I can be excused the occasional social foible or politically incorrect blunder because "I was in a coma." Perhaps the thing I learned is that the brain, even when you're in a coma, grasps for the logic and security of words and sentences and a narrative, even when all you have is fragments and slices of memory, perhaps because there is little logic and safety in the mind when you're there. And that, as crazy as it sounds, there is a *there* there.

Dead Rats and Shrieking Lilacs: Why Blood Smells Better than Pronouns

"Truth," Nicholson Baker says, "smells like Chinese food and sweat." And maybe it does, on some days, but it doesn't smell like that to me. Truth is a decaying mess of a fleshy thing that smells more like a wilting dead thing, and here's why I think so.

It was late September, and I was about to step onto the down escalator with my daughter when, after years of living with only four of my five senses, I regained my sense of smell. It was the closest I'll probably ever come to an epiphany.

Classical epiphanies are those flashes of insight you read about in important books, when—like James Joyce once wrote—"the soul of the commonest object ... seems to us radiant." In Joyce or Shakespeare or whomever, this radiance happens to remarkable characters in remarkable places: to a maudlin Romantic poet looking out at a valley in the Swiss Alps and recognizing sublimity in the life of everything around him, or to a precocious young Irishman who realizes the supreme quality of beauty when he's staggering along a foggy Dublin street at midnight in 1916.

My epiphany happened on a Sunday afternoon on the escalator near the big Winners at Metrotown Mall.

"You smell that?"

"What?" she asked, as if I were calling her out for a fart.

"That smell. What is it?" I stepped onto the escalator cupping an invisible parcel the size of an iPad in front of my chest and, sniffing, angled it at her. "What is it?"

A nose orgasm. My limbic system was registering its first olfactory message in half a decade, and my brain, which for all that time had grown deaf to the receptor cells and sensory neurons sending it those smell signals from the tiny patch of semiotic tissue up in my nose, was scrambling to decode it.

My kid, nonplussed, smiled and looked at the space between my hands.

"Maybe it's popcorn?" We'd just seen a movie. "Or that?" She pointed at a sushi place on the lower level and then at a pizza place.

It was a meaty smell—ample, cooked, and somewhat carnal—but not exactly something you'd eat. The top note was thick, like the pale snap of a lukewarm espresso flavoured with cardamom or something exotic you'd never put in your coffee. But the base note was a seared flank steak marinated in curdled butter milk and wrapped in the dishrag you keep under the kitchen sink.

My kid knew I was more befuddled than usual because of the meds I'd been on for a recent otolaryngological surgery and played along, listing the different sources that were the cause of my "it." Sushi. Pizza. One of the girl stores. The scrupulously body-sprayed teens ahead of us. Pee, which is a common smell in malls. The grease that kept the escalator steps on track beneath our feet. Our feet.

"No." It was an animal smell, oxidized and more musty than musky, and in a crowded mall that could be anything.

I once read about a study that proved that our perception of time is relative to our environment's smell. The scent of coffee makes us think a minute goes by in fewer than sixty seconds, but if we smell baby powder, those sixty seconds feel like a full minute and a half. It wasn't baby powder I was smelling, but that eighteen-second ride down was a stretched recess of raw smell and incarnate words.

Spellbound at the capacity of my nose to smell again but paralyzed by my brain's inability to identify and name what that thing was, I pushed out some adjectives and nouns. *Sweet, sour, smoky, acidy, citrus, burnt, chicken, ish.* Each was an arrow flying at a target but each wavered and dropped off too soon.

That wasn't the epiphany, though. Any linguist can tell you that before we put them into words our perceptions are indistinct globules of mental activity based on fleeting sensations. Nietzsche said words can't attach to the truth of our senses, to the "thing-in-itself," because they're metaphorical representations. Words can't apprehend real things because the essence—of what we see or taste or, in my case, smell—starts disappearing as soon as we sense it, and "there is absolutely no escape, no back way, to the real world." No one in their right mind thinks they can smell a rack of jerk-marinated barbequed ribs by the nasal redolence of the words "citrus" or "spicy," but it's next to impossible to think of sense experiences—especially smell—outside structures that belong to language and not to the empirical world.

Just as there is no connection between a clock chiming the hour and the phenomenon of "time," no direct way from a signifier to a signified, there was no way back to the source of that smell through my adjectives and nouns. Still, that throbbing need to find that one word and attach it to the "thing-in-itself" was distressing.

Sensually aroused but verbally stunted, I was riding that escalator feeling like a kid with a mouthful of Pop Rocks trying to get his dad to stop the car because he needs to pee real bad. Heidegger once said that where words don't come, no things exist. Sure, if you give a name to an "it," the thing it points to might not smell any different, but it will be less uncertain, more factual, than it is with an aloof pronoun. Like any good sommelier knows, you can change a person's taste of wine by using sharp metaphors that, strictly speaking, don't coincide with the sensations of taste or scent but still somehow affect it.

The routine sensations of daily life—the taste of a beer that's too hoppy, the inadvertent eye contact with a homeless guy, the sweaty fingertip that touches your palm when you get your change, the chatter coming from the back of the bus, an undecidable smell on an escalator—never hang around long enough to contain in a word. The historian Simon Schama once gave a lecture where he described opening a letter written in 1799 by a soldier to his wife just before going off to war. The soldier was killed, and his wife, poor thing, died of smallpox before she got it, so the letter was never opened. The guy slipped in a lock of his own hair, which was heavily perfumed, as was the custom back then, and Schama, having opened this "extraordinary musky aroma" that hadn't been smelled for 200 years, says that it drifted to his nose and dissipated, like history itself. "You need to trap it in all its living completeness before it goes."

There's a melancholia to this anecdote of trying to trap an invisible thing that relates to that urge I had to attach paltry words to meaty sensations, to make language dig deep into the dark centre of our sensuous lives and stay there, like an underpaid security guard at a museum. I've never been as relentlessly distressed as I was during the years my nose didn't work, and it was during that eighteen-second ride that I started to understand why.

Five years earlier I was struck with anosmia, which is what the doctors call it when the nerve cells in your nose aren't properly plugged into your brain. I was standing in my garden one August evening—it was all so dramatic—when I realized that the tomato vines weren't leaving that insanely recognizable astringent scent on my skin. I picked at the leaves and covered my mouth and nose like I would a handkerchief but I couldn't smell that archetypal scent of late summer, nor the oregano and Portugal peppers.

The smells died. The erotic aroma of the lilies that always left that yellow powder on my face when I got too close. Grass. My dogs' shit when it'd fill the crevices of my shoes and that sweet residue would follow in my footsteps until it dried and crumbled out. The pads on my dogs' paws, which is the best smell ever. Laundry, clean or dirty. The reassuring familiarity of my daughter's Dove-washed hair. My book-heavy office. A perfumed cleavage. That aroma Al Pacino, in *Scent of a Woman*, calls the "passport to heaven." The having-been-there smell of sheets after sex.

I know a woman who makes her own "smellies" and wears a fragrance necklace. She'd offer her concoctions and I'd lie, say it smelled good, or synesthetically compliment her on how fetching she looks. Same with cooking. Instead of telling her that dinner smelled "good," I'd talk about the taste, but then taste, as I learned during my anosmic years, is a casualty when your sense of smell dies because what we think of as "taste buds" are mostly odour molecules from food that rise to the olfactory epithelium and communicate bytes of food messages to our brains.

Sure, I missed the good smells but, bizarrely, I was more nostalgic for the bad ones. Like the most noxious stench I've ever experienced when I found a colony of dead rats in the insulation behind the basement walls in my old house. It was an unusually hot summer, and there was a garbage strike, and there were a lot of rats in the city. A week or so after setting the poison, I clawed the plywood from the studs and unleashed a fetid paroxysm of decomposing rodent flesh. I swear I felt the smell in my eyes, even heard and tasted it. It was more repugnant than the grim appearance of those six dead rats, their mostly desiccated eyes frozen in the kind of panicked expression at the edge of mortality you'd see in a Goya painting.

The memory of that singularly head-reeling smell of recently killed rat flesh was, during the years my nose was dead, an inscription not only of all the scents I was missing out on but a penetrating reminder that, like those rodents, I was decaying in a descending narrative, one sense at a time. I was dying, which is no surprise, but so too was the world around me, which is. Grenouille, the scent-fetishist in Patrick Süskind's novel *Perfume: The Story of a Murderer*, has no odour himself—"It was as though he did not exist"—and in my case the world had no odour. So it didn't exist, either.

There's this passage in Rilke's letter to the painter Cézanne in which he says that only in the autumn months does the world "let itself be inhaled in one smell." The smell of the "ripe earth" is nicer than the smell of the sea, he says, because it has "depth within itself, darkness, something of the grave almost." What he was trying to say, I think, is that the smell of autumn is ripe, deathly, which is why we like it. Like the smell of dead rats, which I liked. It's not that I was smelling the "darkness," but that I was, with no sense of smell, "something of the grave."

In the sensory realm, we know the physical world only through a neurologically generated, virtual model that we consider "reality." And poetry, and probably most literature, which so often puts into words our failure at ever reaching those hulking Xs we encounter in the empirical world before we descend into death, delivers us from the meaningless corners of sensuous life. There's this poem by e.e. cummings in which the speaker says his mind is "a big hunk of irrevocable nothing which touch and taste and smell / and hearing and sight keep hitting and chipping with sharp fatal / tools / in an agony of sensual chisels." I love how "smell" is at the centre and "sight" at the end of those chisels we use to make our selves because if you ask most people which sense they can do without, most would probably say smell. With each sense—*not* just sight, which has been our go-to sense even before Plato—"i slightly am becoming something a little different."

The poem doesn't really explain my epiphany on the escalator, I know, but it did let me understand how I was, sadly and in such a beautifully sluggish way, unbecoming in a backwards "agony of sensual chisels." Smell and death are related but not just because as we get older we have diminished smell sensitivity. Recently a couple of researchers at the University of Chicago concluded that an adult's inability to identify smells might be an early warning of mortality. The subjects of the tests were asked to identify five common smells—peppermint, fish, orange, rose and leather—and then five years later, in a follow-up, almost 40 percent of the people who had failed to identify these smells were dead. The empiricists tell us we're just the composite of our five senses, which seems about right. So if one of them is deleted we must be twenty percent less, a fifth closer to that state of nothingness where we started.

A week or so before that escalator ride I was sitting in a doctor's office, and he had what looked like a miniature cruise missile in his hand. There was a tiny camera at its end and when he shoved the thing in I could see on his monitor the bone and tissue tucked in below my eyes somewhere way up my nose, which was very cool but also a lot grosser than anything that's ever come out of there before. I know this isn't what the Buddhists call living in the moment or anything like that, but looking at that deficient red and brown mechanism that was responsible for one of my life's toughest passages let me understand, I think, what e.e. cummings must have meant when, in that chiselling poem, he says "hereupon helpless i utter lilac shrieks and scarlet bellowings." It is the exquisitely wretched descent into the final state of sensory nothingness that, as it falls, prompts a resurgence of sensory expression.

When I had my reconstruction surgery to fix the deviation that was denying my smell a few days later, I could have kissed a dead rodent at the odoriferous peak of its decay. After the surgery I sniffed anything I could bring my nose close to, and anybody who would let me. Objects, pets, body parts. Foods and moods, days and atmospheric conditions. I incarcerated each like a psychopathic lover clutches at the object of his desire. I started a list of the scents that were, gradually and by degrees, reanimating my world. The second smell was beer, on a Monday, and then coffee, candy, my own pee, some woman's perfume at work on Friday. On Sunday I was at an Ikea suspended in an aisle where an employee was stocking bins of scented candles. A potpourri of cleansed euphoria, it smelled like being there at the first day of the world. I've never been so happy, not in an Ikea.

As we stepped off the escalator on that too-long descent to the lower level, my daughter pointed to an overpriced candy store that we hadn't been to since she was much younger. It would seem logical.

"Yes, that's it," I told her.

But it wasn't that. I had realized, largely because of the tenacity of that memory of the smell of those six rats, that this, my first palpable smell in all those years was, unsexily and more befitting a mock epic than anything profound, just a large clump of blood that had congealed in my nasal cavity after the surgery. But even blood smells better than pronouns.

No Reading Aloud: Two Book Shelves, a Fig Tree and the Crushing Silence of the Saddest Building in the World

It is always sad when someone leaves home, unless they are simply going around the corner and will return in a few minutes with ice-cream sandwiches.

—Lemony Snicket

"Hey. Look around and take it all in," she says from the top of the front steps, steps that earlier that summer I rebuilt because the rain had rotted the old planks through to the stringers. It was the last meaningful chore I did at my old house before moving across town to the saddest one bedroom in the world, near Granville Island in a building filled with widows, Russians and inexpressive consultant types. It wasn't the kind of place you'd need a rake or wire cutters, but I brought most of my tools, even the big ones. "Because you'll never forget this moment for the rest of your life," she said, and I remember a wistful fatality in her voice, as if she always knew our marriage had to end, was okay with it, but was still taken aback when it finally happened. I know I was.

It was the middle of September, five years ago. I was loading the second of two large shelving units—she kept the two nice ones with the glass doors—into my truck. Half an hour earlier she was helping me carry the first down the steps, but she lost her grip at the bottom near where the root of the Japanese maple buckled the concrete walk, swore and dropped her end. There's still a scuff on the top right of the frame. Frustrated or injured, maybe both, she said some unpleasant things, went back up the stairs and closed the door, which is why I slid the second one down the stairs alone, lift-dragged it down the walk, across the sidewalk and onto the road, tilted and pushed it into the truck alone.

I was securing the two shelves with a bungee cord when she said it. I hadn't noticed that she had come back out and was standing at the top of the stairs. In 1911 when they laid the foundations in this part of East Van they positioned the doors just a spit or two away from the streets, so I'm sure other people heard her say it. It was slightly awkward, yes, but distressingly poetic, too, like a soliloquy of cosmological solemnity announcing itself in a domestic plot twist unfolding on a pleasant late summer afternoon. Imagine Jean-Paul Sartre suddenly breaking out with his "existence precedes essence" exhortation in the middle of a Don Cherry segment on a Saturday afternoon game in December.

When you're standing on the street, emotionally drained from deleting stuff from your house and sweaty from lugging it all into your vehicle so you can start settling in at your new place, and you're aware that the neighbours must be gossiping about what exactly you did to bring about this narrative arc dramatized before their eyes, you don't consider the referential function of all the words that come your way. But if ever a sentence was burdened with traumatic denotation that was it. I was leaving not only her—as bad as it sounds, that was the easy part, because no marriage will withstand revision to neutered daily rapport—but the house with its distant echoes of the history that preceded us and the myths that we made with all the trips to the hardware store, the big chair at the front window where I read, the view of the mountains from the upstairs window and the evening migration of crows, those steps I rebuilt and that she was now standing on, the dogs, my daughter and all those unhurried conversations over breakfast and dinner at the round table, the garage with my hammers, saws and gardening tools and bags of mortar that I would never relinquish to make way for a laneway house, the pond with the bridge made from the back fence I ripped down the first spring there to gain an extra metre of backyard from the alley, my banana plants and fig trees. All of it.

Just not the shelves and my books, and there *had* to be some consolation in that, I thought to myself as I stepped onto the running board to wave a feint "bye" over the truck while trying my best to invoke the nonchalant coolness of Jack Kerouac, who wrote so brashly about "how easy the act of leaving was, and how good it felt."

But Kerouac was wrong. Or half wrong. Leaving felt wretched. I drove up the street, turned right and pulled over under the second chestnut tree at the alley and choked up more than I have at any funeral or break-up or even when the vet gives Owen Wilson a few minutes with his dying dog in *Marley and Me*, but I did it discreetly because I know the guy who lives in the corner house. He's a longshoreman with an F-150. I looked out the passenger window over the three backyards down to the fourth, where both my dogs were probably sitting in the sun, and I saw the bright green split figs through the tall bamboos. When we bought the place, I spent a magnificently dirty weekend digging up the skeletal roots of the bamboos next to the house because they looked like they'd crack the foundation. *My* foundation.

Heidegger has this odd essay in which he contrasts a "building," a place you can "inhabit," from a "dwelling," a place you can "take shelter in." A building always has a dwelling "as its goal." He's talking about something like a sense of "home," that mantle of names and words, memories and stories we cling to, like a mobile library of the imperative self we lug around with us wherever we go because that's who we really need to be in life and that's how, literally, we make any building in which we may find ourselves into a dwelling.

And so a few hours later I was laying out my imperative self to try to make my one-bedroom into a home. Having manoeuvred the shelves against the wall by the window, I drank and, in a disoriented state of spatial melancholy, put my books into place, the sacred novels and books—Purdy, Richler, Baudelaire— on the top shelves of both, literature on the left and theory on the right, and everything on the remaining four beneath. Not only the arrangement of books, but also where the shelves were against the wall, to the left of the window which looked out onto some willow treetops and two adjacent buildings, was an uncanny duplication of the way they were at the house. Italo Calvino says in *If on a Winter's Night a Traveler* that your home, "being the place in which you read, can tell us the position books occupy in your life." Whether they keep the outside world out or just offer you a place to "sink as if into a drug," for example.

With my old Mission rocking chair diagonally facing the theory shelves, a potted Turkish fig tree—which wasn't really a tree but two cuttings I snipped from the root of the mother tree in the backyard earlier that week—at the left arm, and a side table with a low reading light at right, Calvino might conclude that my books signified a purely defensive verbal strategy. It was a hiding place, something temporary that smacked of worthlessness and the general embarrassment of being a middle-aged guy who's devolved from the respectable civic state of home ownership, in which he had abundant shelves and a garden and a garage full of tools and a variety of domestic guy widgetry, to a rootless condition of renting near False Creek. "Oh yes," I could hear Baudelaire saying to me from a hundred and fifty years ago, "this hovel, this home to eternal ennui, is indeed my own." But at least he had the Left Bank in Paris; I was next door to an evangelical seniors' residence on the concrete banks next to Granville Island.

That first night I ate a falafel and rocked and read, no doubt thinking that by some mystic combination of rocking and reading in a patch that resembled my old house, glass of vodka by my side, I could make it feel less like the saddest building in the world. I don't remember what I read but I remember at some point feeling melodramatically sorry for myself and pulling a Czesław Miłosz from the top shelf—because nobody does self-pity and nostalgic suffering like the Slavs—and finding an index card on which years ago I'd written "Language is my homeland." I must have liked the line when I read it when I was a student still charmed by poststructuralism and attached to that adolescent idea that a guy should always be able to pack his stuff—his imperative self—into plastic milk crates that could always double as shelving units. Always be ready to move because wherever you go, as that cryptic mindfulness mantra says, that's where you are. And so on.

But if I wanted to adjust to life in the saddest building ever, I would have to commit to routines and rituals. "Same as you did at your house," Dr. Cheryl told me in her Burrard Street office not long after I moved. "Do repetitive practices, rituals, like every evening at the same time read in the same chair with the same tea." Until then I hadn't really thought of sitting down as a ritual, but only because there was nothing else to do in my little place. There was no place I could use my hammer or saw, and the rake and shovel I brought became museum pieces leaning unusable in a corner of the concrete balcony. I needed an outside to make my inside feel like home. Even with its books and two shelves, the "treehouse," as my daughter started calling my one-bedroom, perhaps because that sounded less distant and absolute, just didn't do it. No grass needed cutting, and there was no dog shit to clean up, so for months after I pulled out of my old house I went back just to mow and rake the lawn, take out the garbage, cut and hammer things. One evening after I took her to a movie called *Crazy, Stupid Love* my daughter pointed out that I reminded her of the Steve Carell character. In one scene Cal drives back to his ex's house in the middle of the night to tend to the yard just because it needed tending. I understood that. My sense of self was entirely bound up with that yard, more so than it's ever been with books.

Then again, even if I had a yard to take care of at the saddest place, there wasn't anybody to talk to about it, to tell just how fast the grass was growing or how gross it was when your finger poked a hole in that little bag and you got dog shit on your fingers. A home "filled with nothing but yourself," like Margaret Atwood says in one of those lines that make me thankful that at least literature can mollify the aching desolation of life: "It's heavy, that lightness. It's crushing, that emptiness."

For a time I started to read out loud to fill that emptiness. I'd read to myself. To myself, out loud, which is psychotic or at the very least childish. The rocking chair sounded like muted barbarism on that white carpet. The walls were thick, the windows were double paned and didn't open—except for the sliding glass door to that sunless balcony where I wasn't allowed to hang planters or have a barbecue—and I heard nothing outside. Nothing. No trucks or sirens, no dogs, no conversations, not even in the hallway, only the irregular vibration of my transplanted bookcases against the wall whenever the garbage chute would slam in the alcove a few feet from my front door. So just my own voice reading Palahniuk or Buday or, when I was well vodka'd up and on the tearful edge of some broody abyss, Schevchenko or Nietzsche. But this ritual of verbal onanism wasn't working. I was making myself into a distraught protagonist in a syrupy Bildungsroman. Libraries are such perfect places but a library where you're the only person reading—out loud—is an aberration. Or an insane asylum. Homes, like libraries, need books and people because both of these, especially when they are together, provide the possibility of dialogue.

Then one evening, a few months in, I happened to get a glimpse of a partially clothed woman walk to her table in one of the adjacent buildings perpendicular to my library wall next to the window that looked over the willows. For many nights afterwards when I'd do my drinking and reading in the Mission rocker at nine or ten o'clock with my "tea" to fulfill that ritual that wasn't working, I'd walk over to the curtain, draw it, and most times I'd see her sitting there. Her profile became a touchstone, though all she ever did was sit there in that all-too-familiar posture of postmodern sociability, hunched over her laptop, face emblued by her screen, drink by her left hand, often a bowl of something on her lap, looking pretty much alone even when she smiled, like she did when she'd get up for another drink thinking, I guessed, of what to type to the guy she was talking to when she got back to her table and slipped into that residual thrum of excitement happening elsewhere in the world.

I imagined her life as a sentence, figuratively and literally, a reflection of my own incarceration at that place, and that sort of became my routine, though I'm sure she didn't have the same malingering night terrors I had grown accustomed to that year. She did little but stare her evenings away into her—no doubt— very good bandwidth and spent hours looking at Facebook, blogs, porn or emailing those who flitted around her world with no lawns to mow or shrubs to trim. I'm sure she was quite lovely in person, but in my voyeur's mind she was a sentence out of Hemingway. Clean, crisp and paratactic in its sublime emotion-lessness. No mess, no fuss, just the pure impact of fingers typing words that were more like statements than invitations to dialogue and audible conversation.

And it was then, somewhere between thinking her robe might just come open on her next trip to the kitchen and speculating about what she really must signify in my life in that solipsism that sometimes opens up when I read and drink alone and shamefully hallucinate that I'm some voice crying out from the wilderness, that it occurred to me that it wasn't just a sense of having made the right decision in my own life I was looking for, it was the sensation that I wasn't alone. A dwelling, a home, has to be hypotactic, a compound sentence at least, or better yet a dialogue where words are spoken in such a way that they require and elicit a response from another person. A dialogue, in other words, not just one-directional statements that are lost in the emptiness of the space in your apartment. Even in the solitary moments, there has to be a voice out there that talks, doesn't just echo back but exists to be talked and listened to. Even when they're not confrontational or argumentative, relationships are, like cutting a fig or building stairs, work. Books help us, and solitude can sure be a salve, but people save us, and doing things for or with them—a chore after work, Saturday-morning hardware-store runs for hinges and bags of mushroom manure, Sunday evening talks during the TV commercials, the purposeful banality of trips to retailers who specialize in faucets or furniture is what makes us. A dwelling, in the Heideggerian meaning, is the feeling of having been there in a dialogue you retain and continue with the one who will be there in the morning and evening, preferably in person, and who wants to talk to you and listen to you because what you both say intersects in palpable ways.

I lived in the sad building for fourteen months and fifteen days, and at no time was it ever home. No matter how much I rearranged the books, no matter what ritual I performed or what I read, either to myself or out loud. Quite the opposite. I took to working sixteen-hour days saying yes to anything anybody asked me to do for them, especially when it meant leaving the "treehouse" and being outside.

Eventually, I moved into a garden suite that is, finally, more like a dwelling, maybe because I have the same bookshelves positioned in the same way and figs, though these ones are out in the sun and rain now, and maybe because I can use my shovel and rakes and hammer if I want to, but mostly because there are people around to talk to in the evenings and in the mornings and I don't need to read out loud here. It's staggering, really, the joy of being aware of other people and having other people be aware of you, isn't it? There's this mysterious character in Hermann Hesse's 1919 novel *Demian*, Frau Eva, who tells a besotted young man who is happy to have finally met her because she will be, in his fragile mind, the source of validation that will tell him what his life is, "One never reaches home," it's just that "where paths that have an affinity for each other intersect the whole world looks like home, for a time." It could be true, in some ontological sense, that we never reach home but those paths, for a time, can intersect. Perhaps only for a time, and perhaps then we need to read out loud, to ourselves, alone.

The Ellipsis and the World Suspended by Some Unique Tear

Grief turns out to be a place none of us know until we reach it.

—Joan Didion

The white bedsheets were folded and laid on the floor by the closet. Sheets folded like that—somewhat frenetically but still, with corners judiciously tucked inside, somehow respectfully—shouldn't ever be on the floor. They weren't laundered. It was a warm afternoon in early June, and by the time I walked up to the bedroom, the sun was coming in through the sliding doors. One of the people had made an effort to fold the sheets so that the stains were gathered into the bulk. That was a kind act, I thought, one I appreciated, even though blood—there was lots of it—has this potent saturation that makes it impossible to conceal in thin white bed linens, no matter how you fold them. And they *looked* heavy, too, still warm and moist with the compressed residue of a life that recently just stopped in what had to be a moment of anguish.

A few hours earlier I was at work, lecturing a first-year class on Northrop Frye's theory of metaphor and myth, and dragging them through the meaning of a single line: "What the metaphor does to space the myth does to time." They weren't getting it, not really, not even with my Taylor Swift examples, but that can be anguish for young minds at nine o'clock in the morning on a Thursday in early June. When my phone vibrated across the table the first time, I ignored it; the second time, too. On the third vibration I turned it over, but when it vibrated *and* rang, I reached for it. My daughter. Another text. "Pops, please!...call."

Some philosophers of language warn against the tendency to assume that elliptical expressions—not the three dots that appear on your phone when someone is texting you but the ones we splice between words in a sentence—are abbreviations of full thoughts. Wittgenstein, who often wondered why people can understand so much more than what's literally said to them in a sentence, pointed out that an expression is elliptical "not because it leaves out something" but because "it is shortened—in comparison with a particular paradigm of our grammar." Staring down at my daughter's three dots on my iPhone that morning, I knew that her emphatic "please," followed by those three little dots, didn't leave anything out but signified an alteration in the grammar of our lives. Emotionally weighty and pointed in its delayed urgency, it was the saddest text I've ever read.

A few minutes later, I was down in my office and I had her on the line. Her distressed tears allowed only two sentences to come stumbling out into her receiver. "Mom's gone. Mom died." That was it. *"Mom's gone. Mom died."* It was this. There's a world in a grain of sand, as William Blake once said, but with a few small words a world changes and becomes a different place.

I don't remember what I said to that. Something like "Wait. *Wait.* What? What?" How else do you respond to that kind of news except with incredulity, as if you misheard because of course the universe would never think of allowing a death to take someone from your world? What I remember is telling her I'd be at the house within the hour, but by then she had passed the phone to an EMT, who explained things to me in the officiously sympathetic language that must be second nature to people in her profession. Rebecca collapsed, they did everything they could for more than forty-five minutes to save her, but she didn't make it, my daughter was being attended by a victim-services officer from the VPD who would stay at the house with the two other constables—dispatched as "standard procedure when there's a 911 call"—until the coroner arrived "on the scene" to do the paperwork and "remove" Rebecca. I asked to speak to my daughter again. The surviving parent is the one who shouldn't lose it, especially the dad, according to the myths and metaphors I know about, so I said everything would be okay and that I'd be there in an hour.

An inexplicable embarrassment followed me when I hung up the phone and went back upstairs to finish my class. For about thirty minutes I pretended not to notice the memories that edged themselves into my head and I deactivated every sliver of nostalgia that threatened to evolve into a narrative and implant itself there, just to avoid the public display of my private emotion. *Steel yourself,* I thought, *push through,* that's what people have to do, even though I knew that that was really just fear and denial dressed up. I talked more about the mechanics of verbal metaphors and tossed out more examples of mythical structures from Taylor Swift songs to lighten the time, but the tides of grief can't be stemmed. We'd been separated for nearly six years, always far better at being close friends than a romantic couple, but we met and got married when we were grad students in English, when I was a theory head and she an unapologetic pop-culture aficionado, so even my Swift schtick was hard, because for the duration of the abbreviated class, I kept hearing the familiar complaint that academics should use examples from what people actually know about to explain the things they don't know and much less care about.

I stopped the class early and went to inform the head of the English Department that I had to cancel the rest of my classes that day, but I didn't want to tell her why, not just then. To "tell" someone that a person who was so very close to me just died, just an hour ago, that would have been what linguists call a "constative utterance," a statement that's either true or false, but my hesitation grew, I'm sure, from the belief—probably because I was scared, still in denial—that saying it would be in some ways a "performative speech act," as if by saying it I was somehow doing it. Not the death, of course, but the grief. The compulsion to express sympathy to a person for someone they've lost—though it's got to be one of the most graceful moments of language, when you look a person in the eye and address their vulnerabilities by enclosing them for a brief moment in your verbal kindness—can be, as beautiful as it is, an unbearably painful gift to receive.

Joan Didion, in *The Year of Magical Thinking*, an elegant text structured to replicate the experience of grief, says we expect to feel shock when people close to us die but that what we don't expect is that the shock will be "obliterative, dislocating to both body and mind." *Obliterative, dislocating.* I didn't know how to act, what to think, or even *how* to think, or if death should make a person think differently at all. Maybe the social conventions of death require nothing but mute sadness.

In reduced-lane traffic I was watching a road crew cut out a piece of pavement near Nanaimo and Broadway, and I remember thinking of Albert Camus, and not just because existentialist books are bibliotherapy for our daily grief, even though I think they probably are. She and I had talked recently about a new translation of *The Stranger* I was using, and she smiled, I remember, when I mentioned the familiar opening lines—"My mother died today. Or maybe yesterday, I don't know"—which is what people who read a lot do when confronted with words of such absurd grace. Remembering that she smiled at the irreverence of those opening words—it might easily have been something from Nietzsche or Wallace Stevens—was a momentary salve.

The nearer I drove to the house, however, the more frightened I became. *Obliterative*. It was the crawling fear of knowing that I would want to speak with her again and again after that—not at that very moment but at many moments in the future, when I'd read something new or reread something old in Camus or Woolf or Pullman, or seen something that referenced *Seinfeld* or *The Sopranos*, or heard something about Leonard Cohen or Tom Waits or bought a new book on grammar history—but that she would remain absent and silent. It's like Frye says in the book I was teaching as she lay dying: the reason we have literature, myth and metaphor is because "underneath all the complexity of human life that uneasy stare of an alien nature is still haunting us." That knowledge that you'll want to talk to someone about something that matters to you so much that you'll want to tell her about it because you know she will listen and understand and you hope she will reciprocate with her own words that skirt themselves onto yours, which will then lead to so many more words and a relationship built on sentences after that, but she'll never respond. That foreboding silence is haunting. It's crying. Even as my complex denials became fears that collapsed into simple fragments and degenerative words—*Can I deal with all this? Who should I call first? Which sister? Family. The funeral. The will. Banks, lawyers. Fuck.*—I was coherently sad.

There's nothing quite as foreboding and unphilosophical as

two police cars parked irregularly in front of your house and an officer stationed at the top of the front steps, the door wide open behind him. Momentarily, I felt like that poor man faced with the apparent power of the apparatus—the police, the bureaucracy, the administration—in Kafka's parable "Before the Law," but when I walked up those steps that I'd built, trying my best to notice that the vines really needed tending and the lawn, too, the uniformed gatekeeper asked if I was the owner. I said "yes" and he replied by introducing himself and offering me his hand in condolence, which I took, and when I asked, choked a bit at his niceness, "Where's my daughter?" he moved aside and pointed in.

It was uncanny. My house, yes it was my house, but it was not, or maybe it was just that it would be the same place but so different from that moment forward in time. All the doors were open or ajar, slightly off, Grizzly the dog who always gets in the way was quarantined in the kitchen, another officer stationed, pistol visible and buttons and badge shining by the refracted yellows, blues and reds from the stained-glass Virgin of Guadalupe window up at the landing where the stairs turn right leading to the bedrooms, and another one sitting next to my daughter and her friend on the chesterfield in the living room beside the bookshelves. I hugged my daughter, and we cried some together and then we sat.

For too many hours we sat there, the police officer from victim services, my daughter and me, at first going over the narrative of what had happened that morning. She got up just after eight, called out for her daughter, who came from across the hall to find her mother sitting, sort of, on the edge of the bed but struggling with her breath and experiencing, no doubt, the breathless fear at the end of life. My daughter exited to phone 911 and came back to find that the struggle had rendered her even closer to the end. She was lying back on the bed. Her eyes were open, but you could tell by the look in her eyes, my daughter said, that she was slipping further away from life. The police and ambulance came. They worked on her for about an hour. But then she just stopped. Hours or days later we talked, my daughter and I, about the fear she saw in her mother's eyes, but that morning we mostly sat, looking out the window to the street and mountains, petting the dog when he wandered in, drinking water to keep ourselves occupied, and idly looking through the envelopes they provided with the documents and pamphlets about death and grief, funerals, expenses and services. Periodically, there were smiles, as there should be, but mostly we just sat, intangibly and fearfully, locked into a moment of silent defamiliarization in a world from which we had been temporarily excused. Who knows? Maybe Didion is right to say that when people lose someone, they "look naked because they think themselves invisible."

There's a passage in a Virginia Woolf novel that she introduced me to when we were in grad school because she knew that I'd like it. And I did, so much so that we used the pages we'd torn from her copy of *To the Lighthouse* as tubular wrappers for the wedding favours we placed on our guests' plates at the reception. In the passage, Lily Briscoe asks Andrew Ramsay what his father's books are about. "Subject and Object and the nature of reality," Andrew says, and then when Lily says she has no idea what that means, he clarifies his point metaphorically: "'Think of a kitchen table,' he told her, 'when you're not there.'"

The coroner was late, about three hours. There was a delay.

An accident or some police incident on Kingsway, I remember hearing one of the police say to another somewhere else in the house when they thought they were out of earshot. I could have gone upstairs, of course, but when I asked to see her, the officer who stood beneath the stained-glass window staring down at his phone said they suggest that people not do that "in these circumstances." The three EMTs and two officers were up in her bedroom for almost an hour. They'd done a tracheotomy. There were effects, he said, and also the condition of the room was less than ideal. He suggested that I not go, and frankly I'm not even sure why I'd asked him, because at the time I don't know if I could have brought myself to see her. *In those circumstances*. So I went out into the backyard with the dog and clipped back some branches from the fig trees and bamboos. From where I stood, looking up at the branches, I could see that the bedroom drapes were open, and someone, either she the night before or one of the EMTs that morning, had opened the sliding door to get some air. I could see the ceiling directly above where she lay dead.

When the coroner finally arrived around one o'clock, the victim-services officer said it would be best for my daughter and her friend to go outside while they "removed" her. It can be traumatic, she said, to see and hear them. The staircase upstairs is visible from where we were sitting in the living room, and the stairs down the front porch are, too. My daughter and her friend exited and leaned against the railing just outside the back door. I stayed and poured a drink, talking to the victim-services officer about the nature of trauma and why she chose this profession, but when I heard the "one, two, three" and the grunts, the wheels and feet move across the hardwood floor upstairs, and the high-pitched metallic clank of the gurney moving over the top steps just up from the stained glass, I went out to the back, too. I drifted back in a few times to see the procedure happen, but I couldn't stay. "The movement of human life," writes Georges Bataille, "tends toward anguish, as the sign of expenditures that are finally excessive, that go beyond what we can bear."

When she was gone, the victim-services officer called us inside. It was about two o'clock. The coroner told us some things and then he shook our hands and left, and then the victim-services officer and the two constables shook our hands and expressed their condolences and then they too left. There were two of us, with the work to come. The telephone calls, the emails, the notifications, the plans, the searching, everything. The beginning of something entirely new can be overwhelming, so my daughter and her friend went downstairs to the consolation of the daybed and computer screen. I went upstairs into her bedroom because I wanted to sit on the bed where she stopped.

She was gone, but not entirely. The place was in relatively good condition at first glance, looking much as it always did—folded clothes on the dresser, the dog bed in the corner, a book with a pair of glasses and an iPhone on the night stand. Reading lamps, one still there from when I slept in that bed years ago and one replacement that she had bought to suit her tastes. A bottle of Tums. *Rocco's Wings*, a fantasy novel for children she'd written a few years ago. The sun was warm and the elementary school around the corner, visible from the back deck, was letting out for the day, so the air carried that universal melody of happy kids walking home. The dog, who followed me upstairs, went out the sliding doors and sat in the sunshine. I sat on the bed, trying to position myself exactly where I figured she was sitting when she first called for my daughter earlier that morning, which sounds weird, but it felt like the right thing to do at the time, though I can't really say why.

In the top drawer of the nightstand, slightly opened, I saw a folder. It was her old Bible-college diploma, the first one she got before her English and law degrees. In the early years, she and I talked often about religion. Her Protestantism, which was formally framed in a diploma because she'd been educated in it, and my Catholicism, which was more about art, wine, and fish and chips on Fridays. The difference, the Biblical scholar I married always said, was that her people were more word-bound to the letter of the text, as "fundamentalists" are, having less tolerance for all the smells and bells and metaphorical language that is pretty much the only thing my people pay much attention to, along with the alcohol. They didn't put Jesus on the cross; they left it empty, which signified for them that he'd ascended or something like that, whereas we left him hanging there, bound and bloodied, a constant reminder of the anguish.

I remember once telling her about a passage from José Saramago's novel *The Gospel According to Jesus Christ*. The narrator is thinking out loud about a painting of the Crucifixion and describing the image of a man who is walking away, looking back over his shoulder and carrying a bucket and sponge. I gave her the novel, and she read the passage, once to herself and then once out loud. "One day, and forever after, this man will be much maligned, accused of having given Jesus vinegar out of spite and contempt when he asked for water, but the truth is that he offered him vinegar and water because at that time it was one of the best ways of quenching thirst." Her eyes watered. I still can't read that passage without the pull of tears that might not be only mine.

Sitting there where she last sat up, waiting for something to happen or not to happen, I wasn't at all sure, I thought about things and looked around. I touched the pillow, the irritatingly soft and ridiculously expensive pillows she'd asked for last Christmas, I leaned over and plugged in her iPhone and closed the drawer, and only then did I notice the bedsheets had been removed. The quilt had been pushed aside, but the white bedsheets, the two that your body immediately touches, were gone, and I was sitting on a mattress. That's when I noticed that the dog had come in from the deck, plopped himself on his bed and was sniffing at the folded parcel of linens.

Of all the evocative death scenes in literature—Dante, Poe, Faulkner, McCarthy—there's only one writer to my knowledge who has described the after-scene aptly. Jonathan Ames, in a piece called "Ron Gospodarski," wrote about a former New York City paramedic who starts a business in the new field of "bio-recovery" because the people the real Gospodarski met on the job were always asking him, "Who can we get to clean this up?" It's something you don't think of much—I certainly hadn't. I mean, it's not only the emotional tenor and enduring history of a room where someone who was your very best friend for so many years just died but, more bluntly, its physical appearance. I just certainly didn't think there would be that many bloodstains on the floor, mostly at the foot of the bed where they must have laid her, but also on the bed, and on the drapes, which are already blood-coloured, but still. I don't know if they did the tracheotomy on the bed or on the floor. I didn't want to picture it, but I did take out my phone and look it up. The definition of "tracheotomy" didn't really cohere with the blood in the room. The mattress itself had no blood on it, oddly, but the bedsheets were red and heavy with her blood, though it was clear that the EMT took the time to at least try to conceal most of it by pleating it inward. That was graceful. My daughter told me that she wouldn't want to go up to the room for a while, which is understandable, so when I was up there that afternoon I took the sheets, which were still surprisingly warm, and placed them in a plastic bag and put them in a utility bin in the back of my truck. The bag sounded loud, too, when it fell against the plastic side of the box, I remember. I haven't thrown it out yet. She's been cremated and there's an urn, but there's also that bundle of bloodstained bedsheets. Maybe it's material evidence of her presence, or a reminder of the anguish one feels at that inconsolable absence. I don't know.

The pull of friendship, maybe more so than the romance of passion, can be sublime, and in its sublimity it can be painful, because one of the two will always die first. The French philosopher Derrida, whose work I fell in love with the year I met her, wrote a book called *The Work of Mourning* in which he eulogized his good friends, most of them writers and academics. I didn't read it fully until recently, because that sort of subject makes more sense when you're in middle age. In one of the essays, he wrote that at the core of every good friendship there's always "the knowledge of finitude." That sense of a time limit on how long we can be friends with those people with whom we share that sacred bond and the possibility of losing that bond are the foundations of all friendship, and we're not talking here about the theatrical "friends" we know from Facebook. Flesh-and-blood friendships, the friendships of looking one another in the eye while speaking, listening and replying. Relationships, the good and memorable ones, can be sustained on language because they are, at their core, entirely constituted in language. "One of us," Derrida says, "each says to himself, the day will come when one of the two of us will see himself no longer seeing the other and so will carry the other within him a while longer, his eyes following without seeing, the world suspended by some unique tear, each time unique, through which everything from then on… will come to be reflected quivering, reflecting disappearance itself." She would have liked that line, I'm sure.

ACKNOWLEDGMENTS

Earlier versions of many of these essays were first published in *subTerrain*, and so a big thank you to the various editors and readers who have worked there over the years. In particular, a special thanks to publisher, editor and friend, Brian Kaufman, who provoked most of these essays by prompting, and also to one-time editor, Dennis Bolen, who introduced me to *subTerrain* and said "culture" happens here. Beyond that, I'd like to thank—and apologize to—the two best teachers I ever had: David Clark of McMaster University and Ian Balfour of York University. Sorry for not pursuing the academic career path as much as I probably should have after grad school.

ABOUT THE AUTHOR

Born in an ethnic enclave of Oakville, Peter Babiak grew up
in Hamilton, Kitchener, and Toronto, Ontario. He studied
English language and literature at the University of Waterloo,
McMaster, and York, and has taught literature, history and
social sciences at a jail for young offenders, contract law and
critical thinking at George Brown College, and economics at
Dominion College, all in Toronto. Peter moved to Vancouver
in 1994 to take an adjunct position teaching English at the
University of British Columbia, where he worked for ten years.
From 2000 to 2002 he coordinated a barrier-free lecture series
and educational facility/book room on Powell Street in
Vancouver's Eastside, and then from 2002 to 2006 he was
Academic Director of Humanities 101, a pioneering outreach
program—the first of its kind in Canada—that brought classes
in the liberal arts, social sciences and "grammar boot camp"
to Vancouver's Downtown Eastside. He has been teaching
English literature, linguistics and grammar/rhetoric at
Langara College for well over a decade.